WALKING

THROUGH

THE FIRE

Nancy Duncan

WALKING

Finding the Purpose of Pain

THROUGH

in the Christian Life

THE FIRE

JAMES R. LUCAS

**BROADMAN
& HOLMAN
PUBLISHERS**

Nashville, Tennessee

Published by Broadman & Holman Publishers,
    Nashville, Tennessee
Acquisitions & Development Editor: Vicki Crumpton
Interior Design: Steven Boyd
Printed in the United States of America

4261-94
0-8054-6194-9

Dewey Decimal Classification: 231.8
Subject Heading: SUFFERING / GOD
Library of Congress Card Catalog Number: 96-15342

Unless otherwise noted, Scripture quotations are from the
Holy Bible, New International Version, copyright © 1973,
1978, 1984 by International Bible Society.

Library of Congress Cataloging-in-Publication Data
Lucas, J. R. (James Raymond), 1950–
    Walking through the fire : finding the purpose of pain
    in the Christian life / James R. Lucas
        p.   cm.
    Includes bibliographical references
    ISBN 0-8054-6194-9 (pbk.)
    1. Pain—Religious aspects—Christianity. 2. Punish-
ment—Religious aspects—Christianity. 3. Providence and
government of God. I. Title.
    BT732.7.L83   1996
    231'.8—dc20

    96-15342
    CIP

96 97 98 99 00 5 4 3 2 1

*This book is dedicated to all who have felt the fire of God,
who have suffered,
who have been stung by the pain of living in a fallen world,
who have sensed God's loving but strong hand on their lives,
and have asked "Why?"*

Contents

Acknowledgments

My first and strongest "thank you" is to Janette Jasperson, whose labors and care have been so instrumental in the development and production of this book. She helped to lay out its format. Her questions, comments, and editing have been of unsurpassed value every step of the way. She has reorganized things that rambled and tightened what was loose. She transcribed tapes and managed to read handwriting that often *I* couldn't read. Her research, which is exemplified in the appendix, proves that they knew what they were doing when they graduated her "summa cum laude" and gave her a Phi Beta Kappa key. Janette, I hope I never have to write a book without you.

Thanks also to Janette's husband, Damon, whose searing questions made me go ever deeper, and whose witty questions kept me on my toes. He has been a wonderful asset throughout the process and is one of those rare friends who is willing to tell a person what he really thinks. Damon, you said this should be my next book—thank you for your early and continual confidence.

As always, the encouragement and input from my daughter Laura has been invaluable. This amazing lady—who managed to graduate with three majors (in education, English literature, and history) just after her twenty-first birthday—was an ongoing inspiration throughout the writing, rewriting, and re-rewriting. Laura, you make being a parent a remarkable pleasure.

I want to express much appreciation to Vicki Crumpton, my editor at Broadman & Holman. She has a wonderful mixture of humor and insight. She takes things seriously and has clear goals but always seems to remember that we human beings are supposed to *enjoy* what we're doing. Vicki, what a delightful experience you made this!

Finally, I want to thank my family, nearby and extended, for their prayers and support. Writing a book is a time-consuming project, but I have always felt the backing of those who are close to me (you know who you are). Thank you, dear ones.

Two other notes. First, I am grateful that God has allowed me to share life with many people, some of whose stories are in this book. I have changed names and some of the details to protect their privacy, but these illustrations come from real, live, breathing, hurting people just like you and me.

Last, many of us involved in this book have experienced a heavy dose of "fire" during its development. I think God wanted to make sure that I would feel it, current and full, before I tried to write about it. This always seems to be His way—putting us through in life what we're putting down on paper. (Janette has told me that she wants my next book to be on the blessings of God.) Thank You, Father, for all Your ways of speaking to us.

Introduction

*E*veryone has faced pain: physical pain, emotional pain, spiritual pain. In the dark, fallen world in which we live, pain is all around us. It's only natural, in the midst of suffering, to cry out for an explanation. *Why is this happening to me? How can there be a God? How can He be good?*

Many books have tackled these questions. Unfortunately, most focus on the creature and his problems rather than on the Creator and His solutions. Instead of using Scripture to shed light on human experience, they use tragedies in the lives of people (many of whom the authors might not even know) as guides for interpreting Scripture.

Walking through the Fire starts from the biblical premise that God is a good, loving Father who protects the way of His faithful ones. No coincidences, happenstance, or meaningless suffering can touch the lives of His children. Instead, in all circumstances He labors for the benefit of those who love Him.

Ironically, the Father's love doesn't shield His children from all pain but instead guarantees that we will face it. How do we know? Hebrews 12:1–13 gives us the answer: "'Because the Lord disciplines those he loves, and he punishes everyone he accepts as a son.'" God's discipline and His punishment are both realities His children will face, probably many times in the course of a lifetime. Even though these things are painful for a time, they should encourage us because they prove that God has claimed us as His own.

Discipline and punishment, often referred to in Scripture respectively as God's refining and consuming fire, are two distinctive threads running all the way through the Bible. Although they can look the same on the surface, their underlying realities are quite different. It is absolutely critical that we distinguish the one from the other, for they come into our lives for different reasons, move toward different goals, and require different responses from us. Much of *Walking through the Fire* is devoted to examining the differences between these two threads—from God's perspective.

All of life is a testing ground for the next. Scripture compares life to a race, a fight, or a great contest. The purpose of the pain of discipline (true discipline is always painful, for "*no* discipline seems pleasant at the time, but painful") is to help us "throw off everything that hinders." We need to do this so that we can run our race in such a way as to win the prize and end up pleasing our Commanding Officer. All of us are hindered in one way or another by old habits and ways of thinking and speaking and reacting. Many of those habits aren't sinful; they're just not *helpful.* God will bring pain into our lives to help us throw them off.

It's easy, when we face the pain of discipline, to become confused and bitter and to complain against God. We can choose to stop running our race altogether, or we can change directions in an attempt to avoid what seems to be causing the trouble. To respond in either way is to lose the blessing of having our "feeble arms and weak knees" strengthened. Resisting or running away from His loving discipline also can invite God's punishment into our lives.

The right response to the pain of discipline is not to stop running our race but to fix our eyes on Jesus and keep going, confident that He will carry us through the trial. If we respond to pain in this way, we will see, in time, the "harvest of righteousness and peace" it produces in our lives. These "trials of many kinds" will bring us to maturity and completeness if we will let them do their work. Then, and only then, will we be able to be grateful for the troubles, which from a strictly human point of view is a ridiculous response.

Punishment, on the other hand, is designed to turn us from the "sin that so easily entangles." Even Christians, who have been redeemed by Christ's blood, will be punished if we persist in sin. We're told that we must "not return to folly."[1] Unfortunately, it's easy to convince ourselves that we're doing better than we really are and to compare ourselves with others. When God's punishment comes, we often rationalize our behavior and rage against God for being unfair, all the while continuing on a sinful path, which is leading to ever more severe judgment.

The right response to punishment is to stop, fall on our knees, and cry out to God in repentance, for only He can free us from the chains of sin. Then, with God's help and power, we must leave the sinful path we're on and again fix our eyes on Jesus. Punishment is an incentive from our loving Father to do just this.

It's critical when we feel the fire to discern whether we're experiencing God's discipline or God's punishment—His refining fire or His consuming fire—so that we can respond correctly. In a very real sense, we should be growing in our faith so we can consistently do two things: welcome discipline (with "pure joy") and be guided by it; and regret punishment (with fear) and do all we can to avoid it. We'll look not only at how to do this rightly, but also why we respond incorrectly and how to avoid the wrong response.

Not only must we make this distinction between discipline and punishment in our own lives, but we must also discern what God is doing in the lives of our family members, friends, and others around us. If we don't see this difference, we could encourage people to "hang in there" when God wants them to repent and change paths. Or, like Job's friends, we could condemn and discourage one whom God isn't punishing, but rather whom He merely wants to "stay the course."

This discernment is available to those who seek it, for God promises wisdom to His faithful ones, and He "takes the upright into his confidence."[2] But how easy it is to give wrong advice without this discernment!

Pain is ever present in a fallen world. Wounds cry out to be healed; wrongs demand to be made right. *Walking through the Fire* offers hope to everyone who suffers, for it shows that God isn't silent, nor is He mysterious and faraway. Instead, His fatherly love is directing all the details of our lives—even our suffering and pain, our discipline and our punishment. He does this to prepare us for great glory and joy when we finally finish our race and collapse into His arms.

Throughout this book, the references for all direct Scripture quotations will either be noted in the text or footnoted, with the reference itself listed at the back of the book in the notes. For those who want to dig more deeply into any issue raised in the book, I am including other pertinent Scripture passages in the appendix. These passages will correspond to the various sections in each chapter. Bible study groups could use the appendix as an in-depth study guide, either by studying the Scripture passages all together or by assigning them reference by reference to different members of the group, who could then summarize their points.

My hope is that this additional Bible study material will help you as you wrestle with the question of why our loving Father in heaven allows pain and suffering in the world He has created. To understand the heart of God, we have to explore what He has said about Himself. Don't believe it because I—or any other author—say it; believe it because God says it's so.

Part One

Basic Principles
of Discipline and Punishment

ONE

But you received the Spirit of sonship.
Romans 8:15

The Fatherhood of God

The Mohammedans have ninety-nine names for God,
but among them all they have not "our Father."

Anonymous

You've just been let out of prison.

You're glad—overjoyed—to finally get out. Even when it seemed comfortable, it never seemed like home. You remember the long years of misery, the panic, the insults, the demeaning treatment. You're ready to shake the dust off your feet and leave this hellhole behind.

You walk down dank corridors and notice, almost for the first time, how foul the place really smells. You can't believe you put up with it. You glance back and forth into the cells as you pass them and can't believe you spent all the life you can remember living like an animal.

You're given a new suit of clothes and led through iron gates into the sunlight. You used to see the same sun in the prison yard, but it never seemed so bright. You stand squinting, getting used to the light, wondering what you'll do next. You think, fuzzily, about who will take care of you, where you should go, and how you can possibly get a job with your record.

Then it comes into focus.

Unbelievable.

You shudder as you take in an elegant, glistening, immaculately detailed limousine in the curved driveway just ahead. You've never seen anything this exquisite. You wonder who it belongs to and why they've come to a place like this. You see the driver come around the back of the car and open the rear door.

Then he turns to you, smiles, and waits.

He's waiting for you.

But you're stuck. You always longed to be treated that well, but you know the car couldn't be for you. This must be some kind of joke.

"Me?" you hear yourself asking. "You're kidding. I don't belong in that beautiful machine! Don't you understand? I'd dirty it up. I'm just a ham-and-egger, a two-bit crook. That getup is first class."

The driver walks over and insists that you get in.

"Go on! I can't afford the fare to ride around in a fancy deal like that. Can't you see I just got out of prison? What's the matter with you?"

He tells you the car belongs to your father.

"Now I know you're crazy! I don't *have* a father. I'm an orphan, see? Nobody ever gave me anything, except the guy who just bailed me out of this horrible place."

He smiles and says the one who owns this limousine is the one who bailed you out.

"You're nuts! This is some kind of scam. Why would somebody bail a bum like me out and then send his *limousine* for me? I'm a zero."

He tells you that his boss must not think so. He really did bail you out and send his limousine to pick you up.

"You're kidding! Really? Why would he want to do that?"

He smiles again and tells you that the master of the grand palace on the hill just adopted you.

You slump to the dusty ground. After a long time, you look at the palace and laugh.

"Me? He just adopted *me*? Now I know you're crazy! Be serious, man! I'm a nobody—always was a nobody. I am glad to be out of prison, though. Glad I took him up on it. Thank him for me, will you?"

The man tells you to thank him yourself.

He lifts you up by the arm. He supports you as you walk, trembling, to the limousine. He whispers gently that you're royalty now, that there'll be no more prisons, that your inheritance is secure.

"What did I ever do for him?" you ask, knowing the answer.

The man affirms your feeling when he says you've done nothing for this one who's just adopted you. Then he shocks you with the starkest of realities: Remember when you pulled the robbery that got you stuck here?

The one who owns this limousine is the one you robbed.

Waves of guilt and embarassment roll over you.

"You're . . . kidding."

"No."

Then fear. "Does he want to kill me?"

"No." He wants to forgive you."

Afetr a pause, you ask, "Do I have to go?"

"No. It's your choice."

It's all become a dream. You try to say something but can't. You decide to go. You slip into the seat and sink into the rich leather. This is too much! You wonder what you'll say to somebody who, after you've robbed him, bails you out of prison and adopts you.

As you pull away, you look back at the austere, silent prison. Then you look ahead at the palace, stunning in its beauty. The absurdity of your good fortune finally hits you. You begin to laugh. A different kind of laugh.

And you never stop.

Who Is This Abba?

The awesome God of the universe is our Daddy.

He isn't *like* a Daddy. He really *is* our Daddy—our Papa, our Father. This reality is stupendous, *almost* incomprehensible.

And it's an even better gift than our salvation.

Being a child of God depends on salvation but goes far beyond it. We could pull a drowning child out of a river, and we would have done something very special. But then to give the child all that we are and have—to make the child a friend and heir—would go far beyond anything that child had a right to ask for or imagine.

Really believing that God is our Abba, our Daddy, is the gateway to understanding the Christian life, including understanding why fire comes into our lives.

One of the questions many Christians ask is whether God really understands them. Does He know who I am and what I need? Does He know when it's best to discipline me with a strong hand in a velvet glove, and when that same strong hand should turn around and pull me close to Himself? Is He able to hold me right there at that balance?

Some people think God is strong but not soft. He's all hammer and pounding but no tenderness and care. Their experience with a tough human father may be the mental model of "father" they transfer to God. God uses a human analogy—"father"—to help us understand Him, but if we associate the two too closely, it can cause us to transfer sinful human nature to God. One dear lady who was sexually abused for many years by her father told me, "God as a Father is a really lousy idea."

If we think God is *this* way, we'll never be able to draw close to Him and relate to Him as a Father who really loves and cares about our hearts. We *will* be able to believe that pain comes from His hand—but this pain will drive us farther from Him, rather than cause us to hide in His arms.

Other people picture God the opposite way. They think He's all softness without strength. They confuse strength with harshness. They think God used to be "tough," back in the days before Christ came, but He's not that way anymore. They're uncomfortable with a Jesus who turns tables over in a temple, whether that temple is in Jerusalem or in the temple of their own hearts.

If we think God is soft but not strong, we'll be totally lost when hard times come our way. We won't understand what's happening to us nor be able to believe that the pain could come from His hand. Nor will we understand or believe that He has the power to take us through that trial.

God is both strong and soft, and He has the two in perfect balance. "For he wounds, but he also binds up; he injures, but his hands also heal."[1] "Though he brings grief, he will show compassion, so great is his unfailing love."[2] If we see that there's no conflict between the God of fire and the God of unfailing love, the reality of His being a Father to us will become ever so much clearer.

Often it's in the trials themselves, when God can seem so strong and hard and even unjust, that we sense our Father's softness. Our life seems to be going well when suddenly we're hit—even blasted—with a trial. It can seem so hard and painful, and we can cry out, "God, You're too strong." But then in the midst of the struggle, we realize that it's the pain itself which God is using to bring us back to Himself and to tuck us under His wing.

After I had been a Christian for about seven years, I became totally "burned out." I went through the motions, went to work, went to church, had a second child. To outward appearances, I was a successful professional and family man. Inside, I was an empty, pain-filled shell. My work became meaningless, even detestable (a subtle but often-used punishment) even as the monetary rewards and recognition increased. Moving to other positions didn't help: I kept having to take myself along with me. My relationships deteriorated, and I was uncertain how to parent. I came home, watched television all evening, and ate my way into a new—and much larger—wardrobe.

For five years I languished until God, through mental, emotional, and physical afflictions, brought me to my senses. He taught me that I had "come" by faith to be saved, but that I was "walking" by sight and human effort. He showed me how to walk in faith and live in victory. He convinced me that He allows "things" to happen to me for my own good, even though it may not feel that way at the time. As I learned these lessons, I eventually came to the place where I thanked God that He had let me live in a pig sty—however glamorous that sty had appeared.

How can it be that the One who allowed me to be afflicted was the same One who comforted me? What an amazing combination!

No Peace without Fire

When we begin to grasp this paradox, we can understand how it is that Jesus can be called the Prince of Peace despite His own claim that He did *not* come to bring peace on the earth. Instead, He came to kindle a fire that would result in the division of even the most apparently intimate of relationships.

What is the fire that Jesus brings? To those who follow Him, Christ brings the purifying fire of discipline, which cleanses the heart of all its dross. It destroys our illusions, which keep us from facing the reality of who we and who others really are. It burns up the false peace with which we've tried to satisfy our hearts, a peace purchased by compromise with sin and the evil world around us. Discipline refines us and matures us.

Dave and Sandra married too young and too soon. They received no premarital counseling, only the classic Christian "blessing": "My, aren't they a nice couple?" The trials came early and in bunches: family members trying to control and direct their lives, differences over childbearing and child rearing, financial struggles, missed responsibilities, hurts from misunderstandings and miscommunication.

Dave and Sandra hadn't sinned by marrying, but the pain of their many trials forced them to reevaluate who they were, their needs, their expectations, and their desires. The lessons were harder and more painful than if they had been patient and explored these issues "up front." But they listened closely to God and absorbed the lessons of discipline. Discipline rightly taken never leaves us with permanent harm, but always leaves us with a stronger spirit—and often with better circumstances.

But to those who love wickedness, Jesus brings the fire of punishment, which, if they refuse to turn from their sins, will eventually consume them.

Jeremy was a young married man who had lived a violent life in the drug culture. He claimed to become a Christian and attended church for a brief time. But he wouldn't let the truth go down deep. (On one occasion, he proudly stood up in a Sunday school class and pulled up his shirt to display a huge, horrible tattoo of the Grim Reaper. Another time he "donated" a lottery ticket to the church—a gift which was promptly returned.) He refused the "little disciplines" along the way. Soon he dropped out of church and resumed his old ways of living. He was eventually shot to death in a fight over drugs, leaving a wife and young child behind—and alone.

Either way, whether we listen or not, Jesus brings fire to every heart. He's the Prince of *true* Peace after the fire, not of false peace without the fire. There is no peace without fire. There is no life without fire. His fire will either purify our hearts or consume them, depending on our response to it.

Most of us would prefer not to believe *this*. We don't want to face God's fire because it burns and it hurts. We want to be able to continue in our illusions and our sin and still have an easy life. We want a false peace—the kind that comes by avoiding confrontation, by refusing to take a stand, by resisting the reality of our own lives—not the real kind brought by the Prince of Peace. We prefer the phony kind because it hurts less in the short run. But it's a peace that is really no peace at all. It leaves our hearts divided—torn in two—and leads to even greater fire down the road.

Only after we've passed through the flames will we realize that the One who baptized us with fire was our Father, the Prince of Peace, and that it was His fire which brought peace to our hearts. This peace is deep-rooted, street-smart, rock-solid. It isn't based on "happy" times or "positive" circumstances. It leaves our hearts whole, put back together. This peace is tied into a distant, unchangeable, and crystalline sea.

Together in the Fire

And then comes another piece of good news. The One who brings the fire is the same One who takes us safely through it.

"Even though I walk through the valley of the shadow of death," the psalmist says matter-of-factly, "I will fear no evil, for you are with me; your rod and your staff, they comfort me."[3]

The reality of the Christian life is that we will walk through the valley of the shadow of death. Have you ever been high in the mountains and noticed the shadow of a cloud moving through the valley below? We can see the sun, and the sunny land, all around the shadow. But when we're down in the valley, those shadows—those clouds—come right over us, and we don't realize that they're moving. Everything around us seems very dark, and we wonder if we'll ever see the sun again. But the clouds *will* keep moving on if we'll keep walking toward the sun.

When we're in the dark valley, it's comforting to know that the Good Shepherd is leading us through it, protecting us with His rod and staff. He wants to pull us through every hard time. If we start to wander off the path and stay under the black cloud, He'll reach out with the crook of His staff and pull us back to His side. And when the wolves try to harm us, He'll drive them away with His rod. It's this certainty—if we'll believe it—which keeps us from overwhelming discouragement and paralyzing panic in the middle of Death Valley.

God is a Father who wants us to be perfect, to "take hold of that for which Christ Jesus took hold of me."[4] He knows the only way for us to become perfect is through tests and trials and purifying fire.

But He's also a Father who "remembers that we are dust,"[5] who knows the limits of our endurance, who has to tell us which way to go because we "have never been this way before."[6] He knows the only way we can endure trials is through His grace and wisdom and power.

Our Firm and Loving Papa

If we cannot—if we will not—relate to God as our Abba, our Papa, the Father that He actually *is*, we'll be confused about the difficulties in our life.

Discipline will begin to look like punishment. Our goal can then become to make the discipline go away. If it doesn't, it will be all too easy for us to doubt, to become angry and bitter, to ask, "Why would God let this happen to me?" If we can do something to make the discipline stop prematurely by compromising, we'll be tempted to take things into our own hands and can end up missing all the benefits of the discipline. Without relationship, we won't recognize the strong side of our Father's heart.

Greg asked to be considered for a deacon's role in his church. In a moment of apparent humility, he asked that anyone who saw things that were amiss in his life come to him and help him "grow." Apparently, he didn't think anyone would—or that he had any real problems—because he was shocked when a number of sincere, loving people approached him about some serious problems. He became extremely defensive, wondered aloud why people were "abusing" him, and attacked those who had come to him. He mistook the hand of discipline for the hand of punishment. He ignored the lessons. His life took a turn toward cynicism and rock-hardness.

On the other side, if we're not careful, punishment will begin to look like discipline. Our goal can then become to persist, to claim the punishment is a "trial," to wear a martyr's face before others. These actions, too, can lead to doubt, anger, and bitterness. We can focus so much on the discomfort that we never see the underlying cause, never see God's probing of our heart and weeping over our sin. Without relationship, we won't recognize the soft side of our Father's heart.

Regina had treated her family as though they were her property. She was demanding, controlling, and nasty. In one of the simplest of human transactions, her family withdrew their hearts from her. They wouldn't give her the "love" she insisted that they "owed" her because of her "position" and all of her "sacrifices" for them. She was being punished by the consequences of her own destructive actions, but she told everyone she met how hard life was and how great her trials were. Her friends, in a misdirected and damaging act repeated countless times every day between friends, told her that they would pray for her in her trial and ask God to soften the "hard hearts" of her family. Unintentionally, they encouraged her to ignore the lessons of punishment.

The God of Balance

I have known few Christians who really know God as their Abba, their firm and loving Papa. It's so easy to see Him as tough, unreliable (although as "good Christians" we would never admit such an ungodly view of God), and unknowable, even though we want Him to be easygoing, to leave us alone (except when we "need" Him), and to tell us only what we want to hear. We can see God as too strong but can want Him as too soft.

Rebecca's view of God involved singing for her church, attending special events, and putting on a "happy face" for other people. She wanted, and believed in, a God of "gooey grace." When God began to call her to go deeper into life and her own heart and to face the realities of her abusive childhood, faltering marriage, and out-of-control children, she balked. She didn't want a God who would allow any pain in her life—and certainly not One who would *bring* it. She concluded, in a discouragingly contented way, "People have to face the fact that I'm basically a superficial person."

Rebecca didn't want a God who holds strength and softness in perfect balance.

But God is God. A God who hammers us, doesn't protect us from harm, confuses us, and leaves us in the dark is not the God of the Bible; rather, that God is a false god—a sinister god of our own imagining, a pagan god. And a God who forever overlooks immaturity and sin, and never brings discipline and punishment into our lives, is also not the God of the Bible. That God, like the first, is a false god.

———

Our God—the one, true God—remembers that we're a "smoldering wick," a "broken reed," and He won't snuff us out while there's any smoke or break us while there's any life. But He always—always—works to perfect us and loves us too much to let us persist in foolishness. Our God is an awesome God.

And He's our Papa.

The LORD . . . takes the upright into his confidence.
Proverbs 3:32

Some First Principles of Suffering

God is great, and therefore He will be sought;
He is good, and therefore He will be found.

Anonymous

―――――

While he was talking with his associates, out of the corner of his eye he saw his old friend coming toward him.

It was a familiar face that he would have recognized even in the dark. They'd gone through some great times together, as their labors expanded profitably and touched thousands of lives. And they'd gone through tough times together, as jealous competitors had set out to destroy their efforts. They had worked twenty-hour days and eaten on the run. They had laughed together and cried together. Few people had been with him in all the ups and downs like this longtime partner.

Suddenly, he stopped speaking. He felt his head jerk, like he'd been slapped. He gasped. He had known a break was coming, but now that it was here it seemed too much to bear. He didn't want the partnership to end. He wanted to plead with this old friend, to tell him how much he loved him, to tell him he'd do anything for him, to try one last time to make it all work out.

But even before they were close enough to speak, he knew it would be no use. This was no accident. This had

―――――

always been part of the plan. He knew his friend wouldn't turn back, and he knew why.

He saw his companion draw close, and he went to meet him. His friend smiled. They exchanged greetings.

And then Judas kissed Him.

———————

What greater suffering can there be than to be betrayed by a close friend—or someone who pretended to be?

Even the death of a close friend is somehow easier to bear. Then we grieve because something that was very good—still *is* very good—has been lost for a time from our daily experience. The friend is gone, but the love lives on.

But when we're betrayed, we grieve because something that seemed to be very good—perhaps even *was* very good—has been lost to us completely. The love is gone, but the "friend" lives on.

This is the suffering that Jesus experienced in the betrayal of Judas. You can almost hear Jesus' questions. Why this way? Why a friend? Why with a kiss? Could it be that God wants us to know that *He* knows the stinging pain that comes from being known, and loved, and at the last, hated?

There are principles to this problem of pain. In this chapter, we'll take a look at some of these important first principles.

Let God Be True

One of the greatest difficulties we can get ourselves into is the I-know-a-person-who . . . dilemma.

The fact is, almost everyone we meet could give us a hundred or more examples of people who were "good people" or "good Christians," who nonetheless didn't get in on an "apparent" promise of God or who had sudden disaster or unexplainable misery fall upon them. These stories lead to the confidence-crushing conclusion that God's promises don't apply to us.

God has given us the privilege of looking closely at who He is. He's even given us the tool, a telescope, to do it. We can gaze through this telescope—His Spirit and His Word—

and see an awesome God in detail, unfathomable to the naked eye. Incredibly, He allows us to see who He is from *His*
perspective.

But a telescope is a tool that can be misused. We can turn
it around and look at Him through the wrong end. We can
move the large end toward ourselves and try to take Him in
from our own perspective. From that orientation, He looks
far away—and very, very small.

What are the results of looking at life through this
"wrong end of the telescope"?

- Life can become a random series of unrelated events—more
  like Las Vegas than a sure inheritance.

- God's promises may seem far off and fuzzy, something to be
  admired from a distance but not claimed—really claimed—
  with unshakable faith.

- What appears to be "disaster" or "punishment" can seem to be
  so unfair, so unjust—even cruel—that our view of God becomes warped, twisted, and confused.

- We can find it very difficult to distinguish between God's discipline, designed to mature us, and Satan's attack, designed to destroy us; or to see how God can even use Satan's assaults as a
  discipline, to see if we will cling to Him and rely on His power.

- Our great God is judged by experience, rather than experience
  being judged by God. Our attitude can become an insult to the
  character of God.

- We begin to reinterpret the holy Word of God through the
  false grid of frail human experience.

- We cover up our confusion, anger, and bitterness with pious
  statements about God's "sovereignty" and "unfathomable
  ways."

- We begin to think that faith is merely resigning ourselves to accept whatever disaster comes our way, believing that somehow
  God controls it, and it will all make sense in heaven—the *que-
  sera-sera* version of Christianity.

What is the cure for this faith-crushing malady?

First, we must say with courage and faith, "Let God be
true and every man a liar" (Rom. 3:4). We must say, "I don't
care if there are *no* examples that 'prove' the Word of God.

I'm *still* going to believe it." We must believe that *all* of God's promises are "yes" in Christ and that He is *always* able and willing to give us exactly what He promises, as long as we meet the conditions. We must believe that He is *perfectly* faithful to those who are faithful to Him.

This isn't "blind, irrational faith." This is the most reasonable faith we can have—to believe someone who never lies. The truly blind and irrational path is to sift through a pile of human experiences—many of them blind and irrational—in a quest for truth. It's like looking for a good meal in a garbage can.

To be able to take this crucial step of faith isn't the whole answer, but rather a beginning. Just because we've decided to trust God doesn't mean we understand why He allows pain in our lives. But we have to start somewhere solid, and starting our journey on the immovable rock of God's faithfulness has no substitute. Later on, this faith will allow us to better understand what He's doing with discipline and punishment. Then it will come full circle, as our understanding of His ways bolsters our faith. For now, even if it seems like an incredible step, join with me in agreeing that God is worth believing totally and that we can do it with His help.

Second, we don't have to think it's presumptuous to go boldly into God's throne room and claim these promises. It's *not,* as some have said, putting our faith *above* God, or "putting our faith in faith." It's choosing at last to have faith, real true biblical faith, *in* the real true biblical God. Faith says simply, "I believe God, period."

A crossroad in each of our lives comes when we face the role of faith as a requirement for successful living and not just for becoming a Christian. Although God gives many "good things" to people without faith—even to the wicked—we won't receive all (or maybe even anything) that God has promised unless we have faith. Many Christians want to be able to doubt God's character and His word but still get in on His promises. God doesn't work that way. It's no more "cruel" to say a Christian will miss out on a promise for lacking faith than to say a non-Christian will miss out on heaven for lacking the same thing.

Third, we can come to understand that examples *illustrate,* but don't *prove,* the Word of God. This is so very, very important. We must *start* with the idea that God's Word is true, and if we can find an example to illustrate it (whether it's a promise, discipline, or punishment), well and good. If we can't find an example, we must still stand on the Word, for ourselves and in our sharing with others. We can never start with an example as our "truth."

We may, for example, never have seen anyone actually follow James 5:14–16 when they were sick. In Philip Yancey's book *Disappointment with God,* although sickness and sick people are discussed at length, no one is ever described as following this passage. In James Dobson's *When God Doesn't Make Sense*—which is full of examples of sickness—only one person is described as following it: Dobson's father, who was dramatically and completely healed—the only person in either book so delivered![1] Coincidence? I don't think so. Here's a knowable biblical truth which contains an astounding promise: Following it "*will* make the sick person well." It's there to be believed and followed—or disbelieved and discarded.

Fourth, we must have the humility to admit that we don't usually know what God is doing with a person, a family, or a situation—and if we're *really* honest, that we don't even *know* most people, families, or situations well enough to be able to reach even a remotely accurate assessment of them.

Robert had a good public image. He attended every church meeting and always had an "answer" from the Bible. People said he was "sweet," "a nice man," "a good husband and father." The reality? He would regularly pin his wife into a corner and, with his bulging face just inches from hers, scream at her for thirty to sixty minutes at a time. He would often spank his children with thirty to fifty brutal strokes, for "serious" offenses like spilling milk. When his wife told others about his behavior in an effort to get help, many didn't believe her. After all, they *knew* Robert, didn't they?

Some writers and speakers use examples of people whom they have never even met to "prove" their interpretation of Scripture. But only God knows those other hearts and what's needed in their lives. How often I have thought I "knew" someone, only to find out later about a horrible sin or problem or attitude hidden from my (but not God's) view.

What are we saying? If we begin with the idea that every scriptural promise means exactly what it says, then we can look for examples—encouraging examples—to illustrate these astounding promises. At the same time, we must always remember that these examples don't *prove* that God always comes through, for God's Word *needs* no human "proof." All we need to know is that when we accurately believe, we will abundantly receive.

But if we start with examples of people who didn't "receive" the results and use these to "prove" that the Bible doesn't really mean what it says, then what are we left with? An empty heart, an empty faith, an empty Bible, an empty God.

I-know-a-person-who arguments may be the most common destroyer of faith. The answer?

Let God be true.

We Can Know and Understand God

Even if we agree that God is always "true," we might feel that we're still stuck because we can't understand what the Bible says.

It's not only possible to know and understand God, it's *mandatory* if we want to avoid discouragement and dysfunctionality. Pain—whether from discipline or punishment—becomes more bearable when we see what God is "up to." Until then, He's like an unexplained physical pain, haunting but not helpful until we seek and find the reasons for it.

What do we mean when we say that God is knowable and understandable? We mean that we can really *know* God. Not by our own efforts, to be sure; but because He communicates to us in His creation, in His Word, and in our hearts—and because He instructs us by His Holy Spirit—we can as Christians really know God. He's our Father, and He *wants* us to know Him.

James Dobson's *When God Doesn't Make Sense,* one of the most popular books of recent years, spends much time trying to convince us that we can't know God. In fact, the author says that trying to know and understand God and attempting to rely on Him to deliver us consistently will actually *destroy* our faith. What, then, is faith to him? It's somehow hanging on to God *in spite of* the fact that He's distant, confusing, hard or impossible to understand, and may let us be wiped out by any or every trial.[2]

But how can we trust someone we can't know and understand, and who may or may not help us when we need Him? In human relationships, we would rightly say that it's absurd to trust such a person. How can we trust God if He acts the same way?

"Blind" faith is not a biblical concept. It's not that we believe in spite of the fact that we're in an unending night; rather, we believe because we *see* the invisible light and are "certain of what we do not see" with our human eyes.[3]

We trust in Someone who defines the word *reliable*. David says in Psalm 22:4, "In you our fathers put their trust; they trusted and you delivered them." We can know from God's Word the kinds of trials that we might face, and we can know from God's Word that He will deliver us. Not might or could—He *will* deliver us.

The Scriptures used in Dobson's book to "prove" that God isn't knowable actually prove the opposite. The author stops a quotation abruptly, before God has even finished the thought. He quotes to the comma but not to the period.

For example, he quotes Proverbs 25:2: "It is the glory of God to conceal a matter." Period. This seems to tell us that God's glory is to hide things from us and leave us in the dark. We *should* wonder about that kind of God. That kind of God wouldn't make sense. But the verse actually goes on to say, "To search out a matter is the glory of kings."[4] Yes, God hides things—so that we can find them!

We're called to participate in the grandest of treasure hunts—heavenly treasure, pearls of great price. Jesus hid these treasures in parables (and God hid them in the recorded history of His people), so that we wouldn't grasp them with only our human understanding but would have to look deeper. The process is to "Ask . . . seek . . . knock."[5] God tells us that we will find Him "when you seek me with all your heart."[6]

Dobson also quotes the first part of Deuteronomy 29:29: "The secret things belong to the LORD our God." But he leaves out the exquisite truth that "the things revealed belong to us and to our children forever, that we may follow all the words of this law."[7] There are some "secret things" that only God knows, things that we don't need to know. But the "things revealed"—through His Spirit, His Word, our conscience, His creation—these things *belong* to us and to our children. *They are our heritage.* We *can* know them.

And he quotes 1 Corinthians 2:16—almost: "'For who has known the mind of the Lord that he may instruct him?'" But he leaves out the last part of the verse, the whole reason why Paul included this quote from Isaiah, the whole point of 1 Corinthians 2:6–16: "But we have the mind of Christ." Glory! We're tiny little beings, yet by receiving Jesus as our Savior and Lord, we gain access to a whole new level of understanding by *having* the very mind of Christ! We don't become Christ or God, but amazingly we "may participate in the divine nature."[8]

What are we saying? Our God is knowable and understandable. He "confides in those who fear him." We don't have to ask someone to go up to the heavens or down to the depths to get the truth for us; instead, "the word is very near you." In Him "we live and move and have our being." "You have an anointing from the Holy One, and all of you know the truth."[9]

We're also saying that Scripture must be viewed in context and balance, and not used in piecemeal fashion.

Finally, our lives, in relation to God and His truth, are also knowable and understandable. Prudence, at its core, means giving thought to our ways. We can understand what God means and expects, and we can discern whether or not we're in line with those expectations. In fact, we *must* discern this, or we'll never know whether or not we're on the right path—whether we should persist in what we're doing or whether we should stop.

The Christian's call is not to blind, confused floundering, hanging on to God even though we can't know Him or understand Him. The call is to know our great God and Father, to understand His intentions, and—by His grace, wisdom, and strength—to walk in good ways.

To know Him is to love Him—and to understand that He's the God of love, not luck.

No Chance

We've talked about the pain that comes from discipline and the pain that comes from punishment, but what about "miscellaneous" pain, the kind that comes out of nowhere and has no real purpose?

There is no such thing.

In spite of the widely-held belief that "junk happens," the reality is quite the opposite. We make choices and—whether we can see the connection or not—those choices often lead to painful consequences. Even pain that doesn't come from our choice—a headache, for example—occurs because we are living in a cause-and-effect universe. Everything happens because of *something*.

This is different than saying that everything happens because it *has* to. God, in His stunning greatness, allows us the dignity of making choices, even while He remains firmly and always in control of the outcomes.

The headache that comes from sinful fretting is a punishment, not just "one more thing" to prove that life is miserable. The headache that comes from someone hitting us is a faith or relational test of the highest order, not "bad luck." The headache that comes from not eating or sleeping properly is a discipline to bring us to balance, not more evidence that life "stinks." And the headache that comes from bumping our head is anything but meaningless—for we can be very sure that God is paying close attention to our response, to see if we'll ask Him to heal the pain or curse Him for allowing it.

At first, much of our pain seems to be just a result of "the way things are," of simple "natural causes." We can assume that a cold is simply something that happens to us in a world filled with germs. But there are no little things. Just because pain isn't a direct consequence of an action doesn't mean that it's not a test of character. How will we respond? Does God really care? We can rest assured that a God who takes note of every careless word, every unseen act of kindness, and every fallen bird cares very much about our response to the tests that "natural causes" bring.

For a Christian there are no "accidents"—no luck, no fortune, no coincidence. There are no accidents of birth, no events that surprise God, nothing in our life about which God is not aware and caring, no decision that doesn't affect something or many things down the road. God *is* in control of the universe. We haven't been left to flounder helplessly in the hands of "fate."

Everything has a cause. Children can suffer because of their parents' unfaithfulness. War can be a discipline or a punishment. We can be hungry as a test of faith, to see if we will cry out to God, or we can be hungry as a punishment for not working or for some other sin. One of the hardest things to do as a human being is to see how our own lives, thoughts, and actions might be causing our own problems.

It's very easy to resist—even bitterly resist—the idea that our own sin or lack of discipline could be the cause of our difficulties and to hate those who try to point this out to us. As Pip said to nasty Orlick in Charles Dickens' *Great Expectations* when Orlick accused Pip of ruining Orlick's name with a girl: "You gave it to yourself; you gained it for yourself. I could have done you no harm, if you had done yourself none."

And everything has a purpose. This is true whether we see the purpose or not. If we love God, we have His *guarantee* that in all things He will be working for our good. There is no meaningless suffering (although there is godly suffering that unfortunately *can* be avoided by compromising our convictions, and needless suffering that *should* be avoided by changing our directions).

God will show us the way we should take. He'll instruct us in the way chosen for us. He'll establish the work of our hands. He'll fulfill His purpose for us. He'll tell us every step of the journey, "This is the way; walk in it."[10]

For our great God and Papa leaves nothing to chance.

Both Discipline and Punishment Are Encouraging

John the Baptist said, "'You brood of vipers! Who warned you to flee from the coming wrath? . . . His winnowing fork is in his hand to clear his threshing floor and to gather the wheat into his barn, but he will burn up the chaff with unquenchable fire.' And with many other words John exhorted the people and preached the good news to them" (Luke 3:7, 17–18).

Doesn't *sound* like exhortation, you say? This is *good* news? But that's what Luke is telling us. Knowing that God will bring discipline and punishment into our lives is good news if we're really interested in our life and destiny. It's only bad news if we're not wanting to grow.

God's Word says, "You have forgotten that word of *encouragement* that addresses you as sons."[11] He then goes on to talk about discipline and punishment. How can enduring pain and trials be encouraging? How can *punishment* be encouraging?

They're encouraging "because the Lord disciplines those he loves and he punishes everyone he accepts as a son."[12] Discipline and punishment from God are encouraging because they prove that we really are His children.

A mother said to me, "Discipline sounds like brutality. It sounds hard and harsh, and I don't think I could do it." And my response to that mother was, "You'd better! The most encouraging thing you can do for someone born with a sinful human nature is discipline her to train her character and punish her to prevent disaster. You have to love her too much to let her be a fool—or to let her be anything less than all God called her to be."

This is why we shouldn't "lose heart" when trials or rebuke come. God hasn't forgotten us—He disciplines and punishes those He loves. It's His love that prompts Him—no, *drives* Him—to do this.

☙

THREE

*For our light and momentary troubles are achieving for us an
eternal glory that far outweighs them all.*
2 Corinthians 4:17

The Fire of God

Troubles are often the tools by which God fashions us
for better things.

Henry Ward Beecher

Jackie's life was coming apart. Her mother had just died, and her older sister was having a nervous breakdown. Her husband wasn't earning enough to support their family of seven, but was so unhappy in his job he was talking about "starting his own business," an idea which terrified her.

Questions flooded her mind. "Why me?" This was followed by the more frightening, "Have I done something to deserve this?" She shuddered as she realized her inattention to God and to her children's spiritual training. Memories of nasty exchanges with her mother spilled over into memories of angry outbursts against her children. She felt guilty and sickened. But then came the loop-closing question: "Would a good God really punish me like this?"

Jackie's dilemma belongs to all of us. It's the dilemma of being a well-intentioned but fallen being. We try hard, but we're not perfect. We do some things right, and some things we really mess up. It leaves us, too, with the basic questions: Is this a test of character? Or am I being clobbered for some reason? These aren't idle questions. When we're alone with ourselves, they are among the most troublesome questions that invade our minds.

These questions revolve around one gigantic biblical idea that has two great strands. The idea is the fire of God.

God Is Fire

The difference between discipline and punishment is the difference between the two fires of God.

The Bible paints God Himself as fire. His body is fire. Fire comes from His mouth and His eyes. His voice comes out of a consuming fire. His throne is ablaze. This God who is our refuge, our Father, is a God of *fire*.

And we're supposed to embrace His flames. "Do not put out the Spirit's fire," we're warned (1 Thess. 5:19). How can we bear to draw near to God and be "salted" with His fire? Because we have His wonderful promise, "When you walk through the fire, you will not be burned; the flames will not set you ablaze" (Isa. 43:2). If we'll choose willingly to walk into His refining fire, we'll find, like Shadrach, Meshach, and Abednego, that our God walks with us, and the only things burned are the cords that bind us. We'll find a clearer vision of God, a closer companionship with Him, and a freedom greater than anything we had ever known before.

If we choose instead to complain and resist and do things our own way, we'll discover only the punishing and consuming fire of God.

We feel God's fire burning when we sin, when someone rebukes us, when we're insulted, when the pressures build, when a friend deserts or betrays us, when we lose our jobs, when a loved one gets sick or dies. It's all fire. We feel the heat. We don't like it, but we can't escape it. And it's totally critical that we learn what to do with its two blazing strands.

The Fire of Discipline

Everyone has faced pain—physical pain, emotional pain, mental pain, spiritual pain. Pain is all around us. It can be so intense and consuming that we feel like we're wading through a bog in an oppressive swamp. Oswald Chambers said that a person will never be able to deal well with this life until he faces the fact that it is fundamentally tragic. In itself, by itself, the world is a pretty sad place.

We hear about tragedies all the time. Newspapers, radio, and television seem to thrive on them. Tragedies lead people to ask, "How can there be a God?" Or, "If there is a God, how can He be good?" If we just look at the world through human eyes, it's a valley of the shadow of death, with trials and pain—from moderate to murderous—surrounding us.

And these trials come in many forms and in large quantities. We're told to "Consider it pure joy when you *fall into the midst of* trials of many kinds."[1] We, of course, would rather have them come one at a time and in very small doses—if they have to come at all. But God has a different curriculum. This includes intensive testing now, which will help us be victorious in a critical time, perhaps twenty years into the future.

I had a lot of pain as a child. When I was seven, I almost died from kidney disease, hypertension, and hemorrhaging in my brain. I missed so much school that I couldn't even keep track of it. One morning around Christmas I woke up under an oxygen tent. I can remember the terror and how hard it was just to breathe. And I remember everything hurting. At a very young age, I learned deep lessons about the fragile nature of life and what a gift each day really was.

I also had major problems with my teeth. I can remember times when the dentist had to cut away a whole tooth except for four "points" at the corners. He would then put a band around it and fill it with silver. This procedure was indescribably painful, but it happened so frequently that I learned not to respond to the pain.

Through those and other experiences, God taught me a lesson which I have only fully understood in recent years. There is a lot of pain in life, and complaining about it doesn't make it one bit better—although it does make our relationships with God and others a whole lot worse.

And even as tough as it might be, physical pain often seems small compared to emotional, mental, and spiritual pain. This "invisible" pain takes few, if any, forms as challenging as the loss of a family member or close friend. I experienced this with the death of my father in 1981.

My dad ("Lefty" to his friends) had lost connection with his children. He worked at two jobs seven days a week until I (the oldest child) was fifteen, when he borrowed the money to buy his own business. As that venture soured, he began to drink heavily, bottoming out with abusive behavior toward the family and massive liver surgery shortly after I went away to college.

He left home and lived in one room in a boarding house. For several years I was so angry with him that I could hardly stand to see him. We reconciled in 1976, although it was hard right to the end to talk with him about things of the heart. It killed me to watch this man, who had once gotten a scholarship to Vanderbilt University, spend his days watching television game shows and working crossword puzzles.

Finally, his liver, his kidneys—his whole body—failed. The last time I saw him alive he was bloated and yellow, with a tube down his throat and tears pouring from his eyes. He wanted to talk but couldn't because of the tube. Even though I had no tube, I couldn't talk either. He hadn't hugged me since I was a little boy, and now he would never be able to do it.

My mother called me in the middle of the night to tell me he was gone. I cried into my pillow through the rest of the night. Somehow, I held myself together through the time in the funeral home and through the funeral itself, even when I placed several meaningful items in the coffin. Only later, as I went through the possessions in his room and found information about a trip to the mountains that he'd planned for years but would never get to take, did my heart and eyes explode.

Did this crushing pain bring me any benefit? At the time, I would have said no. It was overwhelming, discouraging pain that made joy seem irrecoverable. Mainly it just hurt and hurt and hurt. It didn't even cross my mind that I might ever stop crying.

But some way, somehow, I did stop. And then I began to sense things, to feel things, to know things. I learned to go as deep as I can, soon and always, with everyone of importance in my life. I saw the need to live a balanced life, planning in much time for relationships. I perceived how important it was to talk about real things, heart things, with my own children. And I had the importance of a hug—a meaningful hug—implanted in my soul. In some incredible way, over months and years, the pain taught me to become what I wished my father had been.

Hardships Are Integral to the Christian Life

The Bible gives us both an encouragement and a sobering description of the Christian life: "Then [Paul and Barnabas] returned to Lystra, Iconium and Antioch, strengthening the disciples and encouraging them to remain true to the faith. *'We must go through many hardships to enter the kingdom of God,'* they said" (Acts 14:21–22, emphasis added).

It's clear: If we're going to "*remain* true to the faith," we're headed for "many hardships." What's a "hardship"? It's "suffering or privation difficult to bear." In other words, it's a test, a difficult test. Most of us don't want that. We squirm at and resist such a thought.

And yet the Bible says: "We *must* go through many hardships." To do what? "To enter the kingdom of God." Our mothers had to go through hardship for us to be born; so must we, as part of being born "again." Being born again isn't a quick and easy switch to a new form of life. There's pain and crying and blood.

Paul calls us to "endure hardship . . . like a good soldier of Christ Jesus."[2] What does a "good soldier" do with hardship? He accepts it, understands it, and prepares for it. He undergoes training to outlast the enemy. He grits his teeth, stands up under the hardship, and refuses to buckle under the pressure. He purposes to learn all he can—about life, trials, the enemy, and himself—so he can endure. He uses weapons—divine weapons—to fight the enemy.

And when the moment of truth comes, he wins.

Sources of Painful Trials

Trials can come from a number of different directions:

- *Persecution.* A missionary once said that being a missionary would be easy if he didn't have to deal with people! Many of our trials will come from unjust suffering inflicted on us by other people—including those who claim to be Christians.

- *Loss.* Other trials come from the loss of those we love, or from problems that burden them and us. Paul talked about being saved from "sorrow upon sorrow" when a loved one was delivered from death. This is not to say that God might kill somebody to test us. There are promises about living longer by living God's way. But the loss of even an aged friend whose "time has come" can bring an aching pain.

- *Bad Decisions.* Some trials come from bad decisions—not sinful decisions, but flawed decisions that show poor judgment. Maybe we didn't check everything out, and we've ended up involved in an organization or a relationship or a deal that causes us great pain. This pain is a discipline designed to hone us, but it results from our faulty decision.

- *Facing the Truth.* Choosing to face the truth can be a source of pain. This can mean facing the truth about an abusive parent or spouse, a poor career path, misplaced trust in someone who uses our vulnerability against us, or our own weaknesses.

- *Being Alive.* Choosing to be alive and grow can bring real pain along with overflowing joy. Paul said that he was "sorrowful, *yet* always rejoicing."[3] Laying aside old unsinful but "comfortable" relationships or habits that are "permissible but not beneficial" and putting new people or disciplines in their place can be anything but painless.[4]

- *The Evil One.* Last, let's not forget the Evil One, who delights in bringing pain. The prime mover behind the trials of Job and countless others, his mission seems to include bringing upon people some fraction of the pain which he himself faces in a doomed eternity.

The Invitation of Discipline

It's so easy to wish that discipline would go away. It's very, very human to resist the pain that comes with discipline, the pain that's inseparable from the fruitful, powerful, joyous life. Discipline by its very nature is challenging: "*No* discipline seems pleasant at the time, but painful."[5]

But pain is an invitation to growth. It's our Father's way of saying to us, when we're wallowing in our flabbiness, "You don't have to stay that way, you know. I have a plan that will make you into something incredibly special and useful. But it's going to hurt. Please accept this, and please don't run away from it. There's no other way."

We can rest in several certainties. We know that the discipline will be no more or no less than what we really need. We know that He will keep His promises. And we know that we will not be harmed.

I have to be disciplined. If I'm wise, I *want* to be disciplined. I want to be disciplined because I don't want to be a baby for the rest of my life. I want to be disciplined because I want to have the strength to survive and win in the many future, but now unseen, battles of my life. I want to be disciplined because I want to live a life that amounts to something. I want to be disciplined because I don't like the alternative of living like I'm not a son of God.

Discipline provides, in its very presence, an opportunity to grow. If we see discipline (and the pain that always accompanies it) for what it really is—a critical part of the path to spiritual maturity—then at last we'll be able to make sense of the command that at first reading sounds so absolutely absurd: "Consider it pure joy when you face trials of many kinds."[6] Why? How can we do this?

Because we know the good that comes from facing trials well. We *know.*

The Fire of Punishment

Ted felt good about the conversation in Sunday school. He had led the group in a discussion about God's "unconditional love." He had told the class that as Christians, "we can no longer be punished for our sins because Christ already took our punishment for us." When one woman asked him what happened when Christians sinned, Ted told her that "we just have to turn it over to Jesus."

Ted didn't feel quite so good about the conversation he had in the hall afterward. One of the deacons had told him that Nelson, a longtime church member, was getting too "cozy" with Jenny, a married woman. They had been seen talking "intimately" in a "corner" and laughing together. As

Nelson passed him in the hall, Ted felt questions, and even a little resentment, arise in his mind.

Christians are often caught between two opposing ideas. It's amazing how we can try to hold both of these ideas in our minds at the same time.

The first idea is that a Christian can't be punished, that becoming a Christian eliminates that threat. After all, didn't Christ take our punishment for us on the cross? In an age of cheap grace and little understanding of God and His ways, we might assume that we can do whatever we decide, because punishment no longer plays a role in our lives.

But there's another idea, a disquieting thought, a nagging proposition that somehow won't ever go completely away. It's a simple thought: clear, precise, intimidating. It goes something like this: "Do not be deceived: God cannot be mocked. A man reaps what he sows."[7]

This thought tells us several important things, not the least of which is that we can be deceived about this whole matter of punishment. In what way can we be deceived? By assuming that our lives can mock God, and yet somehow we won't reap what we sow. But whether we try to fool ourselves or not, we *will* reap what we sow.

There's another truth that undermines our attempts to excuse our behavior: "It is time for judgment to *begin* with the family of God."[8] It's not just that God will punish His children as well as others. Because sin is so repugnant to Him, His punishment *starts* with His own children.

What is punishment? Punishment is defined as "the measure of suffering justly inflicted as a retribution for wrongdoing." It comes as a result of sin.

Surely, God is "gracious and compassionate, slow to anger and abounding in love."[9] But He can't be mocked. He *won't* be mocked. Ted, the Sunday school leader, was mocking God on two fronts. In the first place, he was "selling" a god that doesn't exist, a god who doesn't require justice in the lives of Christians. In his zeal to present the mercy of God, he confused relief from eternal fire with relief from the principle of reaping what we sow.

In the second place, Ted mocked God by listening to the gossip about Nelson. The same man who said God wouldn't punish Christians for their sins began in his heart to punish Nelson on the basis of—nothing. We human beings are amazing: We can excuse those whom God will not, and we can condemn those whom God will not.

This is one of the plagues of our day, a false view of God which carries over into our relationships with people. On the one hand, many preach a "cheap forgiveness," where we're to forgive someone who offends us even if they're unrepentant and would do it again. At the same time, we can buy into hearsay, gossip, and slander, and reject and condemn people who have never offended us. We can tell the woman who was raped to forgive the man who would gladly do it again, while we hold close to our hearts nasty thoughts about a person who has done no wrong.

Anytime we're too soft on sin or too hard on sinners, we mock the God who rules the heavens.

God never allows sin to go unpunished. He puts up with our rebelliousness and our hardheartedness, but only for so long. Then, for the sake of justice, He has to take action. "A God all mercy," said Israel Zangwill, "is a God unjust."

Eventually God will bring things to an irresistible moment, either when the sin becomes such a burden on the sinner that he repents and God forgives him, or when the sin becomes such a burden on God that it reaches its limit and God finally finishes him. This point can be reached in an individual's life (like Ahab and Jezebel), a family's life (like Eli's), the life of apparent believers (like the Jews in the desert), or the life of a whole nation (like the Canaanites).

Do we—does anyone—have the right to complain when punished? Jeremiah tells us *no:* "Why should any living man complain when punished for his sins?"[10] The dead don't complain—they *know* without question that they're getting what they deserve. It's only we, the living, who can delude ourselves into thinking we're really doing well and that the punishment we're receiving isn't really just.

But spare us from believing that all we need is justice. If God were to treat us as our sins, and our laziness, and our indifference deserve, we would all be in very serious trouble. Instead, we should try to see God's fatherly, punishing hand, in order to do what Jeremiah calls us to do in the very next verse: "Let us examine our ways and test them, and *let us return to the LORD.*"

And there is really no excuse. "Now what I am commanding you today is not too difficult for you or beyond your reach. . . . No, the word is very near you; it is in your mouth and in your heart so you may obey it."[11] All of our excuses pale next to this simple, unarguable truth.

There are only two alternatives to the process of self-examination, self-testing, and returning to the Lord.

The first is to refuse to see these things clearly, to blur the difference between discipline and punishment, to superficially compare ourselves with others, and to deny that there's something amiss in our lives. This refusal will lead to confusion, discouragement, and depression that no amount of counseling will dispel.

The other alternative is to play the fool, to complain and rage against the Lord, even while our own folly ruins our lives. If we stay deliberately confused long enough, we will always end up ruined. We invite more punishment and wrath and, eventually, God's consuming fire. It's a very bad place to be.

But we don't have to end up there.

Punishment Is Built into Life

Punishment is built by God into the very order of things, into the laws of the creation. So often we can think of punishment as something "inserted" into life from an outside, invisible world. Punishment can come in that form, but more usual is the punishment that's "built into" the sin.

War is such an example. Although every nation seeks to justify its wars, and Christians can all too easily wrap the flag and patriotism around the Bible (and wrap the Bible around political decisions), war is generally a judgment on one or both sides. God used the Persian Empire to punish the Babylonians, after the Babylonians had punished the Assyrians, after the Assyrians had punished the Israelites. (The others got in on punishing the Israelites too.)

The list could go on and on. Lust advances to guilt, shame, exposure, and disease. Greed, which is idolatry, leads to poverty and shame. Anger destroys all care and affection from others. Laziness produces poverty and scarcity. Gluttony causes self-worth and emotional problems and can lead to an earlier death. Drunkenness destroys the liver and the mind. In a very real sense, when we sin, we punish ourselves.

There's no escaping the relentless concept that punishment is built into life. And God doesn't play favorites. His system isn't the arbitrary legal system that human beings so often construct. Man's system will release an evil man after a major offense if he happens to be rich or famous, while it will put another man away for twenty years on a minor charge if he happens to be the wrong "type." Not so with God. "He will reward each person according to what he has done."[12]

In a widely-discussed book, the author agrees that war is an example of punishment that can come upon a people for their sins. In the very same chapter, however, he denies this principle in the issue of AIDS, which he assures us in no uncertain terms is *not* a punishment for sin. Why the difference? Because, he says, "innocent" people are killed by AIDS. But isn't that so in war as well?[13]

A sobering truth about punishment is that innocent people do often suffer. The misery that comes from punishment can be handed down to our physical and spiritual descendants, causing our children to suffer for our actions. The Lord told those who disobeyed Him in the desert: "Your children will be shepherds here for forty years, *suffering for your unfaithfulness,* until the last of your bodies lies in the desert."[14] Even if they don't claim the sins as their own and "earn" their own punishment, they can receive a spillover effect that will cause their hearts to groan.

Why would God allow this to happen? At least in part as a lesson to the innocent sufferer. "These things occurred as examples to keep us from setting our hearts on evil things as they did."[15] Our sinful nature is bent toward evil, but we can respond wisely and soberly when we see others being punished. The truth stands: "Flog a mocker, and the simple will learn prudence."[16] If innocent suffering leads to wisdom, it's really a blessing disguised as injustice.

And the good news of Scripture includes the truth that only the "soul who sins is the one who will die."[17] Punishment to the third and fourth generation only continues upon those descendants who choose, like their ancestors, to hate God. We can suffer because of someone else's actions, but we're punished only for our own. The children of Israel were released when the last of the previous generation laid down in the desert and died. The descendants went into the land. They paid attention to the punishment of their parents and so avoided it themselves.

Unless the innocent party "buys into" the sin, his suffering takes the form of discipline, not punishment. The parent's punishment is the child's discipline. We might not think the child's suffering is "fair," but God alone knows what discipline we need to find Him and to follow His better ways.

There is, of course, no guarantee that the suffering ones won't become the punished ones. Abused children can grow up to become abusers. Gluttony, drunkenness, greed, lust—all get passed on as inheritances. These are ugly balls and chains, difficult to escape, horrible in their increasing devastation, and demanding ever-greater punishment—until someone finally says "enough" and reaches out a desperate hand for Jesus.

Anger is one of these dreadful heritages. Robert was full of rage and abusive thoughts. These spilled over into hateful tirades against his daughter Molly. Over time, Robert's rage caused his heart to deaden and rot, a fearsome punishment all by itself. Molly—as always happens—closed her heart to him, which brought to Robert the further punishment of isolation and alienation. Then, as she grew older, Molly began to rage angrily at Robert, which brought his actions full circle and yet another measure of punishment on his head.

Of course, it didn't stop there. Molly began passing the anger and abuse along to her brothers and sisters. Her suffering became their suffering; the victim became the victimizer. Without a change, Molly would have treated her own children the same way. Some child 200 years from now could reap some of the awful crop sown by Robert in Molly's heart.

But Molly chose instead to break this "chain." She listened to God and His Word and began to sense that something was amiss. Her mother and pastor and others were honest about Robert's abuse, so Molly could know the truth and have it set her free. She learned ways to rid herself of this terrible inherited disease. And she avoided punishing those around her with this sin that had, perhaps, already worked its harm for ten or fifteen generations. Molly won.

Punishment is built into life. Punishment can be handed down. But we can end it here.

May it stop with us.

Sources of Punishment

Punishment can come from a number of directions:

- *Sin.* In a sense, all punishment originates with sin. If we persist in sin, we will be punished. We must work with God to eliminate sin from our lives. We want Him to be able to put His arm around us to protect us, rather than lifting His arm to spank us.

- *Pride.* Pride is a sin itself, but it also works as an "insulator" against other sins. "In his own eyes he flatters himself too much to detect or hate his sin."[18] Pride sets us up as our own god and turns us into a controller or manipulator of others. It believes it has a better idea than God. Pride *always* leads to destruction and a fall.

- *Willful Ignorance.* Scripture speaks of the simpleton—the naive, immature person—who walks blindly into disaster. Ignorance, according to the Bible, may lessen the punishment, but it will never eliminate it.

- *Folly.* One writer has called folly "wooden-headedness." It's characterized by not giving God room in our thoughts; not learning from experience; not listening to advice; ignoring the growing resentment of those around us; putting ourselves first; and believing that we're doing "pretty well" in spite of the evidence. The essence of folly is to keep doing the same thing over and over again while hoping to get a different result.

- *Lack of Faith.* Sin isn't just a wrong action; sin is, in fact, anything that doesn't come from faith. God tells us that He "does not let the righteous go hungry," but if we refuse to believe it, then we can go hungry, or even starve to death.[19] This is real punishment, even though we have never stolen food or cursed God.

God, a grand Father, does what any good parent will do. He explains things clearly to His children so they know without question or confusion what brings blessings and what brings punishment. He gives warnings. He's consistent. He plans the best time for the punishment. He matches the punishment to the offense in degree (and often in kind) and knows when we've had enough. As much as possible, He lets natural consequences serve as the punishment.

Last and not least, He does it all in persistent hope that His children will mend their ways—so that He can mend their hearts.

The Invitation of Punishment

This truth is so simple and yet so freeing: *I don't have to be punished!* Disciplined, yes; punished, never!

If we walk with God carefully, listening and doing, adjusting and maturing, we don't have to be punished—not once, not for the rest of our days. Glory! *Glory!*

This isn't because we're Christians. As we've already seen, we can be Christians and still be punished. Rather it's because we're paying "more careful attention . . . to what we have heard, so that we do not drift away."[20] We're told to be "very careful" how we live.[21] If we truly love and obey God's Word (and don't just claim to), we can have "great peace . . . and nothing can make [us] stumble."[22]

A word of warning is necessary. God can deliver us now and still punish us later, if we stop walking in faith and let sin creep in. This is why we're told, "If you think you are standing firm, be careful that you don't fall!"[23] He won't take away our salvation, but He can punish us severely and take away everything else.

But the choice is ours. Thomas Bernard said that our sense of sin is in proportion to our nearness to God. We won't see how black our own hearts are if we're not close to God and immersing ourselves in His Word. The easiest person to deceive is always the one we see in the mirror.

But God is never fooled.

Let's not let ourselves be fooled either. Let's draw close enough to God that we can see sin as sin and avoid it. Let's live with our ears pressed against His heart, and we'll never have to be punished again.

Latch onto this truth. Let it sink in. I don't have to be punished. I don't have to be punished, because Christ already took the blows for me. I don't have to be punished, because Jesus lives to give me the grace to say no to sin.

And yes to a way of life that needs no punishment.

Making Sense of the Fire

Ultimately, all fire makes sense. It *always* makes sense—even if we might not be able to see it at that exact moment. We don't live in a random creation where God can be mocked, trials have no meaning, and punishment has no point.

Seeing this truth—that the meaning is there, in the invisible realm—is one measure of faith. "Blessed are those who have *not* seen and yet have believed."[24]

If it's a trial, the pain and affliction can't be ignored. We have only two ways to react. If we persevere by faith, we'll eventually see why it is happening and give thanks all the more. If we won't persevere—the choice is ours, even though the grace to do it is His—then we may *never* see why; we'll only grow angry and bitter and rage against the Lord, and eventually turn the discipline into punishment.

If it's a judgment, misery and destruction cannot be ignored. Again, we have only two ways to react. If we hear God's voice in it and repent and make restitution, we can go on to victory. If we won't hear God's voice in it and instead persist—if we try to call His punishment "discipline" or dismiss it altogether—we'll bring ever-greater devastation on our heads, and eventually "will suddenly be destroyed—without remedy."[25]

Discipline, no matter how hard, we must learn to welcome with "pure joy." Punishment, no matter how light, we must learn to avert with trembling fear.

Part Two

The Refining Fire
of Discipline

F O U R

Surely he took up our infirmities and carried our sorrows.
Isaiah 53:4

Jesus and Discipline

He has seen but half the universe
who never has been shewn the house of pain.

Ralph Waldo Emerson

*T*he woman rushed into the room. She saw her sister slumped on the floor in the corner and heard her profound sobbing.

The events of the previous days swept through her mind. Their brother had come down with a serious illness. They had sent for help, but it hadn't come in time. They had had such confidence that God would be gracious to them and that their brother would be restored to health.

But four days ago, the end had come. She had sat at the foot of the sweat-filled bed, her sister sitting near him, ear pressed against his mouth. "I love you," she had heard him saying to her sister. "I've never known any woman who was more passionate or God-fearing than you." Then he had painfully turned his head away from her sister to face her. "And you, my dear—your care for me brings me so much joy." He smiled, laid back, and closed his eyes.

And he was gone. She had felt numb, unable to move. Then she had heard her sister begin to weep—at first softly, and then welling up to the moaning and sobbing that, after four days, had not subsided. They had talked during that time and had felt their grief increased by the shared feeling that if help had arrived in time, the disaster could have been avoided.

She closed her eyes tightly to erase the memories. "Sister," she said softly to the crumpled bundle in the corner. "He's here."

Her sister didn't look up but tried to choke down her sobs—she knew the "He" her sister was describing. "I . . . I can't . . . move," she breathed in a raspy whisper. "I . . . just can't."

"Won't you come with me?"

Her sister looked up. "Why?" she snarled as she pushed her rumpled hair back from her wet face. "What good . . . what could I say to Him?"

"Don't be angry at Him, Mary," her sister said gently. "There must have been a good reason why He didn't come."

"Good reason! *Good reason!* Don't tell me about your 'good reasons.'"

"You know how much He loves you."

"If He loved me, He would have come."

"He's come now."

Mary looked up, confused and frantic. "Oh, Martha," she said, shaking her head, "He can do anything. He's healed so many strangers. We asked Him to . . . come. He told us He loved us. He said we were like family to Him." She buried her face in her arms. "He didn't even come for the funeral!"

Martha walked over and put her hand on Mary's head. "You really believe in Him, don't you?"

Mary looked up, her eyes desperate. "Yes, I do." She paused. "I did." She shook her head. "I don't know what I believe." She cried again.

Martha started to speak but decided it would be useless. She turned and walked out of the room. Mary heard her sister's footsteps fade into the dining area beyond.

Later, Mary felt a hand slip under her arm. "Mary," she heard her sister whisper in her ear, "let's get away from here." Martha helped Mary to her feet and led her into the small back room, away from the friends who hovered near them. Mary sagged to the floor. Martha knelt down in front of her.

Martha caressed Mary's face in a vain attempt to wipe the streams of tears away. "Mary, Mary," she said tenderly, "the Teacher is here." Mary looked away.

"I don't care."

"Mary, I know that isn't true. I know how much you care about Him."

"Not any more. I'm . . . I'm through. . . ."

Martha moved closer and patted her. "He's asking for *you*," Martha encouraged softly.

As soon as Mary heard this, she jumped to her feet. She was electrified but disoriented, as though she wanted to run but didn't know where. She rushed out of the room, through the other rooms, and into the street beyond. Others, surprised, began to follow her.

But Mary never looked back.

She ran as fast as she could, stumbling, crying, moaning. She tripped and fell hard to the ground. She picked herself up and, without thought about the dirt on her face and clothes, began running again. She pulled up her dress so she could run more freely. "Jesus, Jesus, Jesus," she kept saying to herself. "Help . . . me. Help . . . me. Oh, Jesus, Jesus, Jesus!"

Then she saw Him standing in the road that led into the village. Somehow, she knew that He was waiting for her.

She never stopped running. As she came within inches of Him, she looked down and fell at His feet. "Oh, Jesus, my Jesus," she groaned. "Lord," she pleaded, grabbing His feet, "if you'd been here, my brother wouldn't have died."

Jesus looked down at her wild hair and filthy clothes. He felt her warm tears on His feet. And He loved her. He felt— what *were* those feelings? Affection, compassion, care? Yes, but more. He saw others coming up the road. As they saw Mary at His feet, they too began to drop to the ground in tears.

What *are* these feelings? He had never felt such a rush, such a mix, of emotions at the same time. He wanted to reach down and comfort her, but He couldn't move. He clenched His fists, and His whole body began to tremble. His heart felt sick, broken, anguished. His throat tightened, and He struggled to swallow. He felt His teeth clench.

What *are* these feelings?

Then He knew. Pain. Gut-wrenching, heartbreaking, relentless pain. Unbearable, unimaginable pain. He felt it coursing into Him from the uncontrollable wailing and intense grasping of the intimate friend at His feet. He sensed it almost flying through the air from the mourners strewn about the road. Torture. The pain of affliction.

He looked at one of Mary's friends nearby. He was surprised at how difficult it was to speak. "Where have you laid him?" He breathed more than asked.

The woman He had spoken to rubbed her sleeve across her face. "Come and see, Lord," she said as she slowly rose to her feet and began to walk.

But Jesus couldn't move. He wanted to, He felt the urgency to do it, but He couldn't. He stood there, transfixed, numb, helpless. And then He felt it, rushing up from deep inside Him: sighing, moaning, burning, shuddering. What *is* this? He felt more: choking, breaking, a desire to scream.

It came pouring out of Him. It started as a broken shout, but trailed off into a shattered wail. Something in Him wanted to hold it back, to control it, but He couldn't do it. He gave Himself up to the river of agony. He cried, He choked, He groaned, He shook violently. The grief of the woman at His feet had become His own.

Now He knew.

John, in chapter 11 of his gospel, shares the story of a little family who let themselves get wrapped up with Jesus. Mary, Martha, Lazarus—the story seems so familiar, gets talked about so often, even gets into the *Jesus* movies. It's the story of a miracle, one so great that life around Jesus would never be the same. A man who was dead and in a tomb for four days is raised up and given back to his sisters.

The story begins with Jesus getting the word that Lazarus is sick, but He chooses not to go right away. Astoundingly, He waits until Lazarus is dead. He tells His followers that He delayed "for your sake . . . so that you may believe." We know that, from our perspective, one reason for this incident is so that we might see His power and know that He can raise us up too.

But there is more, much more, to this story. To be sure, Jesus delays so that they and we might see His glory; that much is clear. But this One who "shared in their humanity . . . had to be made like his brothers *in every way*, in order that he might *become* a merciful and faithful high priest."[1] Part of this agonizing time was for us—but the rest of it was for *Jesus*.

He had come to share in our humanity, to be—incredibly—made like us in every way. That includes experiencing pain—real, deep, heart-wrenching pain. Why? Because *we* have pain: we have to face pain, see pain, respond to pain. He did this so that He could feel human pain, our pain. He wanted our pain to be His pain.

He had to do this, the Scripture tells us, so that He could *become* a merciful High Priest. Do you feel the strangeness of that truth? Jesus was and is God. How could He have to "become" anything? How strange! But there it is. He came so He could go through the same feelings and struggles and misery and *become* merciful. There is a large difference between knowing about pain and experiencing its searing heat in your own human heart.

"When Jesus saw [Mary] weeping, and the Jews who had come along with her also weeping, he was *deeply* moved in spirit and troubled." He feels and shares her pain firsthand. He senses her inability, her reluctance, to come to meet Him; this is relational pain, the kind that tears hearts to pieces. He waits outside the village for her, asks for her, and watches this disheveled woman whom He loves run desperately to Him and fall helplessly at His feet.

He tries to take it all in. It overwhelms Him. He's "deeply moved in spirit and troubled." He weeps so uncontrollably that those around Him see it as representing a very great love for Lazarus. They think He's crying because He's just found out that Lazarus is dead. But please note that He's not crying for Lazarus. He already knows that Lazarus is dead; He's known it for days, but hasn't cried until now. In fact, He knows that He's going to raise Lazarus from the dead, and that in the meantime Lazarus is in Paradise. Perhaps He feels some pain for Lazarus, but that's not what makes Him weep.

He doesn't begin weeping at the tomb. He weeps with Mary, for Mary, wrapped up with Mary. He feels her pain so deeply that He stands immobilized and groans. Her broken heart breaks His. One of the reasons why this extraordinary event takes place is for Jesus to feel human pain—Mary's, Martha's, the mourners', His own. He cries for Himself, as He feels the pain of being a human being in a very broken world. And He cries for and with the living, with their pain deepening His own.

This experience of pain helps Him to understand our pain, our grief, our desperateness. He speaks to us in our pain. He starts by asking for us to come to Him, as He did when He stayed outside the village and asked Mary of Bethany to come to Him. Or He simply and tenderly says our name, as He did when He appeared to Mary Magdalene.

His experience with Mary of Bethany helped Him to understand Mary Magdalene's pain later, as she sat numb and weeping outside His tomb after His crucifixion. He knows from experience that sometimes we can't move because of our pain, and we need to hear Him ask for us or call our name. Glory, hallelujah, Jesus understands our pain!

And He speaks these words into the pain of those who love Him: "I will rescue him. . . . He will call upon me, and I will answer him; I will be with him in trouble, I will deliver him and honor him."[2] He raised Lazarus from the dead and restored him to Mary. Her pain turned to joy and gratefulness. John records her astounding and passionate act of pouring expensive perfume on Jesus' feet and washing them with her hair.

She took abuse for this wild act of gratitude and worship—from Jesus' own followers. But she didn't care. Her pain had brought her so much closer to Jesus that her reputation and what people thought seemed as nothing in comparison. She had experienced pain beyond her ability to understand or cope, but Jesus had come. He had delayed and let her suffer, but He had come. He had come, and He had delivered her.

If we wait on Him, trust Him, hold onto Him for dear life, He will come to us and deliver us as well. He will *always* come.

Always.

FIVE

*Know then in your heart that as a man disciplines his son,
so the Lord your God disciplines you.*
Deuteronomy 8:5

God's Willingness
to Discipline

Count each affliction, whether light or grave,
God's messenger sent down to thee.

Aubrey Thomas De Vere

*W*e should make no mistake about it: Our God is willing to discipline us.

Something in us wishes this wasn't so. As fragile beings, we don't like pain, which is very understandable—but not very helpful. Until we realize and accept the fact that our Father is willing to discipline us, we'll never be able to comprehend what He's doing in our lives.

"I have tested you in the furnace of affliction," He tells us, matter-of-factly.[1] We can resist and resent the heat, but our God doesn't. The heat is where He tests us and challenges us to become something more useful. God wants to "fire" us—so we can become better employed.

A glass former takes rods of glass and forms them into exquisite designs—swans, sailing ships, flowers. The key element in the process is heat. The master performs his delicate work in the center of a blazing flame. He wears special glasses which enable him to see even tiny details in spite of the blinding light.

This is how God is with us. He holds our life in His hands. He delicately shapes our form in the center of a blazing flame—the furnace of affliction. He misses no details as He uses our trials and pain to form a sumptuous masterpiece. "Come then, affliction, if my Father wills, and be my frowning friend. A friend that frowns is better than a smiling enemy" (anonymous).

The glass*blower* adds the element of air. Objects are formed by forcing air into molten glass, which produces a hollow sphere. Keys to success include the air pressure, angle of the pipe, and the cooling speed of the glass. Tools are used for shaping as the pipe is twirled. The glass is reheated as required to make for easy forming.

This is another way of looking at how God forms us. Only when we're "fired," only when we're softened, can the "air" of His Holy Spirit do its best work in filling us. As we begin to take shape, God knows just how much air we need, how to hold us, twirl us, work on us, cool us, and reheat us. Glass—beautiful, useful, and fragile—is formed.

A third picture is of a clay vessel, molded into a useful and perhaps beautiful shape. The major ingredients of success include the proper composition of the clay and the potter's skill in shaping the wet material. But the most important ingredient is firing the vessel at the correct temperature. It's unusable and easily deformed until it's put into a furnace and "fired." The heat is what gives it its strength, its ability to achieve its intended purpose, and its only way to maintain its form. This last crucial step depends on the skill, judgment, and experience of the potter.

So it is with us. God, the Master Potter, is the one who put us together; He knows our frame. And He's working on us all of the time, shaping, molding, forming, finishing. He knows what to do with us even when we don't. But no matter how ready we appear to be, until we're "fired" we're not usable for the Kingdom. We have no strength, no enduring structure. We'll soon be a formless lump of clay once again. God has the skill, judgment, and "experience" to ensure success in our finishing.

These pictures illustrate the "firing processes" which God is willing to use in His disciplinary plan for our lives. One of these is forming fire. The other is finishing fire. Together they are what the Bible calls "refining" fire.

Forming Fire

Many truths come as part of a process, where the heat is used throughout and not just at the end.

Quite a few years ago, God gave me a fresh, new love for His people. I had "burned out" but was now ready once again to care for His sheep. I was able to see people's brokenness in a clearer, more tender way. I felt—for the first time, although I'd been a Christian for years—what Jesus must have felt when compassion filled His heart for people who were "like sheep without a shepherd."

So I poured myself into people. I invested my time and energies in them deeply—not just preaching and teaching and counseling, but climbing into their boats with them and trying to be a faithful friend. Even though my life (both as a non-Christian and a Christian) should have told me otherwise, I waded in with the assumption that if I loved people deeply enough, they would be healed and grow—and love me back in the bargain.

Then came the forming fire.

First was the teenage girl who seemed to be so needy for a friend. I began to teach her and encourage her. I took her out one-on-one for hamburgers and sharing. I took her to seminars that I thought would be useful to her life. Her mother, in thanking me, said, "Everyone loves you, Jim."

But everyone didn't. Her daughter didn't. A time came when she had done something very foolish. I took her aside and gently but firmly shared with her how what she'd done could bring her devastating harm. She thanked me by rejecting me totally, tearing me down with her peers, and making faces at me behind my back. No attempt at reconciliation could pierce her animosity.

Then there was the young married couple who practically lived with us for two years. They were in my home three, four, five nights a week. We shared Scripture and labor, joy and sorrow, ministry and life. The husband once told me that he would trust me with his life and the lives of his wife and child. The time came when he assaulted me verbally without cause (except for his admitted jealousy), spit on our relationship, and walked away.

These experiences—and others like them—hurt beyond description, and I can still feel the fire. But God used this pain—the intense, piercing, enveloping, I'm-going-to-hide-under-my-blankets pain—to show me some very important truths: Many people will return evil for good; like Jesus, we should give our time to many but our hearts to few; we should rejoice when we're treated this way ("because great is your reward in heaven, for that is how their fathers treated the prophets");[2] we should be careful where we spend our few precious hours and invest them with discernment; and in spite of hatred, exclusion, insult, and rejection, we must continue to offer ourselves as a "living sacrifice," just as Jesus did.

The alternative to learning these lessons was to waste my life—either by withdrawing and spending it on personal interests and pursuits or by continuing to give my heart to everyone and having it be demolished. Either course would have built up my resentment against people and God. These lessons—from God's forming fire—were painful, at times unbelievably so, but how necessary they were for me to be the whole person God wants me to be.

And how necessary they were to teach me to persist in loving people, even though some will—like Judas—kiss me and kill me in the same breath.

Finishing Fire

God often shows us things in the same way that a teacher instructs his student. He brings in appropriate people, books, articles, circumstances, and Scriptures to teach us new or deeper truths about Himself or life. We begin to see that our earlier, simpler version of truth was incomplete. He highlights for us a more penetrating reality.

Then, when we've "got it," when the forming fire has finished its work, the finishing fire comes.

God brings this fire into our lives because He knows that we really haven't "got it" when we have the form but not the strength. Seeing a new truth is not the same as really *knowing* that truth. We can acknowledge the accuracy of a teaching and yet still not apply that teaching to our life. Finishing fire is God's indispensable tool for developing perseverance.

Hannah was living a "comfortable" life—she was living in an illusion. Outwardly she seemed energetic and happy. Inside she was dying. She used many things—movies, food, humor—to hide from the truth. Then she began to see an ugly but all-too-common reality, the reality of sexual abuse. At first she read about it because she wanted to help other women, but slowly she realized that the symptoms fit her own heart. As she discussed her feelings with those she trusted, she began to acknowledge that this may have been part of her life story.

Hannah came to see the truth about abuse, its effects, and its symptoms. Then came the finishing fire, as God looked at the molded form of her life and knew she was ready to receive a new life strength. Hannah began, without being prompted by counseling or hypnosis or drugs, to remember the abuse she had suffered for ten years from her father. She filled many pages of a journal with the repulsive details.

The fire was very, very hot and burned deeply into her soul. The illusions about her father and home life melted away in the blazing heat. The thought patterns and habits she had developed to protect her "little girl" heart from pain, once a necessary approach was now limiting her growth, turned red hot and evaporated. She cried and grieved and wailed in the furnace of affliction.

And then God took her out of the furnace. The memories are clear, the grief is real, but the lovely clay vessel is stronger and more durable. Hannah knows the truth in the deepest of ways, and it has truly set her free. She had deadened her heart; the pain was a sign that life was returning and was God's way of making her who she is today—joyful, alive, courageous, and very strong.

Pain Is an Ally

Did you know that God gives us pain as a gift?

In the physical realm, this truth is obvious. If we didn't have pain receptors, we could leave our hands on a hot stove until we smelled something burning. If we had cancer but felt no pain, we wouldn't seek treatment until it was too late.

Pain is not only an indicator that something is wrong; it's also a sign that growth is taking place. Children can grow so fast that their legs ache from the changes. I remember as a child the relentless "growing" pain that left me helpless and crying. I've watched my own children experience the same thing. We parents rub their legs with soothing salve. We tell them that it means they're growing and that nothing is "wrong."

The same phenomenon can happen in the spiritual realm. Our hearts can stretch to love another or to give up illusions. This too can hurt, but it's a pain that comes from growing to maturity. And our Father is there to rub our hearts with soothing salve.

Pain is an ally. Many believers have been sold the lie that Christians won't face troubles and trials and purifying fire. They've been told that becoming a Christian somehow means that all of a person's problems are over. Jesus, on the other hand, said, "In this world you *will* have trouble." There's no way to miss it. We can cling to the rest of the verse: "Take heart! I have overcome the world." But it doesn't change the fact that we will have trouble.[3]

The "cheap" version of Christianity fails to realize the simple principle that, as one man said, "Hot fire makes good steel." If we want to be Christians who are as strong as steel, we're going to have to face some hot fire.

All of Life Is a Testing Ground

"Therefore, since we are surrounded by such a great cloud of witnesses, let us throw off everything that hinders . . . , and let us run with perseverance the race marked out for us. Let us fix our eyes on Jesus. . . . Consider him who endured such opposition from sinful men, so that you will not grow weary and lose heart" (Heb. 12:1–3).

The writer of Hebrews says that every Christian is running a race with great throngs of witnesses—the heroes of the faith who have already reached heaven—watching and cheering us on. This race is a marathon, not a hundred-yard dash, and the racecourse is full of things that will slow us down or trip us up. It's an obstacle course, with barriers to climb and holes to jump across and vines and webs everywhere that can wrap around our legs and bring us to the ground.

To successfully run our marathon, we have to throw off all the weights we're carrying around. These weights might not be sinful, but they'll hinder us nonetheless. If we try running an endurance race with a two-hundred-pound sack on our back, we'll never finish, never win. How do we "throw off everything that hinders"? That comes through the pain of discipline. God will bring trials into our lives to help us get rid of those weights.

One "weight" might be the area of plans and follow-through. Most of us have not been trained to prioritize our plans and then "work them" in priority order. The result is that we flounder around, unfocused and unproductive, frittering away our time on "urgent" things or things that are "easy" to do. Discipline could take the form of a missed deadline that causes career pain, a missed appointment that causes relational pain, or a missed opportunity that causes soul pain. If we pay attention, examine the pain and its cause, and avoid complaining about "fairness," we can learn a lot from this discipline.

The writer goes on to tell us that to run our race effectively we have to run with perseverance, fixing our eyes on Jesus. If we look at the storm and the waves, we're going down—at least until we look to Jesus again. If we look only at Him, contrary to human logic, the waves become a sidewalk to a more mature faith. The *essence* of faith is to continue looking at the only One who can make a difference in the middle of a typhoon.

Let's fix our eyes on Jesus, "who for the joy set before him endured the cross, scorning its shame." The reason Jesus set aside His glory was because He could see the joy on the other side. Was there joy in being crucified? No. So where was the joy? The joy was in rescuing you and me.

By His work on the cross and our faith in that work, Christ pulled us out of the fire of judgment. He ignored the shame and the brutality of the cross because it was of little consequence compared to the joy set before Him in heaven. If we fix our eyes on Him, we'll make it through the trials, see true victory, and have a real, battle-hardened joy that beats the phony "let's smile and laugh and pretend we're happy" version of Christianity a hundred times out of a hundred. We'll also see that the joy waiting at the end of our race is far greater than any trials we could ever face.

And we *will* face many trials. All of life is a testing ground from start to finish. It's officers' training school for the ages to come. Will we run our race in such a way as to win the prize, or will we quit before the end? Will we fight the good fight, or will we flee when the enemy attacks? Will we persist until the war is won, or will we give up after—or during—a particularly fierce battle?

If we can't stand the heat, how can we stay in the kitchen? If we can't run with the big dogs, how can we get off the porch? "'If you have raced with men on foot and they have worn you out, how can you compete with horses? If you stumble in safe country, how will you manage in the thickets by the Jordan?'" (Jer. 12:5).

Job understood the ongoing nature of this testing: "'What is man that you make so much of him, that you give him so much attention, that you examine him every morning and *test him every moment?*'" (Job 7:17–18, emphasis added).

Job's conviction, unlike what so many have said, is not that God is off somewhere far away, ignoring us. Job's conviction is that God never leaves us alone—not for a morning, not for a *moment*. "A man's ways are in full view of the LORD, and he examines all his paths."[4] God leads us into deserts to test us, to humble us, to know what's in our hearts, to find out whether we're going to keep following Him no matter what.

Like Christ, we face trials and pain in our race. And unlike Christ, we can "grow weary and lose heart" to the point where we collapse in the middle of the race. We can let the pain of life and relationships discourage us from pressing on. We can be disqualified for the prize and lose what we've worked for. Sooner or later, giving up can seem like a reasonable solution.

If we don't give up, though, there will come a time when we can collapse. After some runners have finished a great race, they take a step or two more and then crumple. They've finished the race, and now they can relax and rejoice. Someday we'll finish our race, and as we break the tape and fall in a relaxed and collapsed heap, where will we land? Right in the arms of Jesus! Jesus is at the end of our course, waiting to catch us as we cross the line.

That's the time to rest. But not now.

Some Trials May Go Away; Some May Not

Some disciplines are short-term disciplines, some are middle-term, and some are long-term. God will bring some tests in for ten days, as He did with Daniel. Other tests will go on perhaps for months and years, as Jeremiah found out in a dungeon and a cistern.

Regardless of how long they last, God "knows how to rescue godly men from trials." [5] In fact, even if someone has "many troubles, . . . the LORD delivers him from them *all*."[6]

Christians can be led down two wrong paths about troubles and deliverance. The first, which we discussed earlier, is that becoming a Christian will somehow free us from all troubles. But "everyone who wants to live a godly life in Christ Jesus *will* be persecuted."[7] The second wrong path is the teaching that God may or may not deliver us from the troubles that do come. But He promises us over and over again—at least seven times in Psalm 34 alone—that He will deliver us from *all* troubles and fears. *All.*

Yet we as tiny beings can be so time-conscious that we can end up being time-bound. Deliverance has to come within a certain period of time or there is no deliverance—or so we can believe, and so we might then act. "I prayed earnestly for three months and wasn't delivered, so it must be that I'll just have to accept the situation." Three whole months! "Better a patient man than a warrior," Solomon says.[8] Why? Because a warrior is ready to act, which is good; a patient person is ready to trust, which is better.

There is only one kind of trial from which we should *not* want to be delivered: a trial related to our calling, our purpose, our ministry. If the only way to be "delivered" would be to give up our position, to compromise, to turn back, then we should delight in the midst of the ongoing trial instead. Paul had one, a trial related to his position as an apostle and writer of "surpassingly great revelations."

There were "others [who] were tortured and *refused* to be released, so that they might gain a *better* resurrection."[9] The ultimate example was the God-man who prayed that the cup—the cross—before Him might be taken away, yet committed Himself to God's will. That He chose not to be delivered is the reason you and I can have joy.

Discipline: God's Unchanging Plan for People

As you read through the Bible, it becomes very apparent that God carefully disciplines those He loves. At times, it seems like those who are closest to Him get the most discipline. People like:

Joseph—a man richly blessed by God, who was sold into slavery by his own brothers, sold into prison by a lying woman, and sold into obscurity by an inconsiderate prison mate. He went through years of this before he reached the position God had planned for him. In fact, he had to go through years of this to be ready for the position God had planned for him.

Joseph's life illustrates the fact that we might have to go through a long series of trials to be ready for our great moment of success. Another is that we might not see fully what God is doing until we near the end of the process.

Moses—the most humble man on earth, a chosen leader, who was forced into anonymity for forty years because he stood up for a fellow Israelite. He was ignored and mistreated by Pharaoh and driven to depression and frustration by the very people he was leading.

We see from Moses' trials that being humble won't keep us from being accused of pride. Caring for people won't keep them from abusing us. Being a good example doesn't mean that very many will follow it.

David—a man after God's own heart, anointed king of Israel right before he was driven into hiding and hunted like an animal. He was mistreated by his brothers, by Saul, and by his own wife.

David's life shows the absurdity of the view that being a believer will shield us from hardship. It also shows that being a believer doesn't mean we will have no conflict with people who are "close" to us.

Paul—who was given "surpassingly great revelations," and along with them was beaten five times with thirty-nine lashes and three times with rods, was stoned once, was shipwrecked three times, imprisoned frequently, and "exposed to death again and again."[10]

We see in Paul the consummate follower of Christ who, because of following Christ, took abuse that most of us can't even imagine. All of us want the "great revelations," the mountaintop view of God. But do we want the great pain which may accompany it?

The whole Bible is full of this kind of story. Why? Because God's loving plan is full of suffering. We can respond wrongly to it or we can resent God for it, but we can't change Him into a God who won't discipline us.

He loves us way too much for that.

SIX

My comfort in my suffering is this:
Your promise preserves my life.
Psalm 119:50

Ten Purposes of Discipline

God who gives the wound gives the salve.

Miguel de Cervantes, *Don Quixote*

Anne was caught up in a war beyond her understanding. Her father had, in a blind rage, perjured himself before a judge about Anne's mother and had gotten sole custody of the teenage honor student. This hypocritical monster then began to abuse Anne verbally, emotionally, and physically. Social service was called in and removed Anne from her home, but, because of the judge's custody orders, couldn't return her to her mother, whom she loved. Anne was placed in foster care, where she felt lost in confusion and despair. She wondered why a good God would let such a thing happen.

Gradually, Anne learned what God was doing with all that pain. During the separation, her relationship with both God and her mother became even more special and enduring. God doesn't bring pain because He enjoys afflicting His children, but because He's a loving Father who knows that we need those trials so that we can grow up and grow deep. Scripture lists many different reasons why God allows pain to come into our lives. Let's take a look at ten of them.

1. To Teach Us to Listen to God

Sometimes we get so busy and preoccupied with the details of life that we have a hard time hearing God speak. God will bring discipline into our lives so that we'll tune out the noise around us and focus on Him and His goals instead.

Bruce had been on an "upwardly mobile" track in his career. He had made a good income and had achieved outward success and recognition. Then he went to work for a boss who didn't like him. After three difficult years, Bruce was fired—a traumatic, life-upsetting event.

But Bruce decided to view it as a trial—a test to be passed—rather than as a disaster to be survived. The following months became a sabbatical gift from God. Bruce looked in many directions and listened closely to God. The result was a career path that met Bruce's needs more completely than he had ever thought possible. If he had instead grown bitter and hard of hearing, the outcome could have been much different.

Habits can prevent growth, and they can be very hard to change. When God wants to give us a clearer truth and direction for our lives, He often sends the message with fire so we'll be sure to pay attention. When He told Moses to return to Egypt and lead the Israelites out of bondage, He didn't appear in a vision or a dream or in human form. He appeared in a burning bush. God came to Moses with fire, and Moses got the point.

After the psalmist experienced God's fire, he came to the amazing point of saying, "It was *good* for me to be afflicted so that I might learn your decrees."[1] He said that he was *glad* God had disciplined him! The discipline had been painful—he calls it an affliction. But in retrospect, the joy of hearing God speak to him outweighed the pain.

The enemy would like us to think that when God speaks to us in fire—in fiery trials, hardships, problems, or challenges—it means our life and ministry are over. Instead, God wants to give us direction and truth in the midst of the pain, which will take us to better destinations and a more effective ministry.

Probably the first thing we should do when we face a trial is to stop and listen to God. We need to ask, "God, why are You bringing this pain into my life? What do I need to learn from You?" As we mature, we withhold our conclusions until we've heard all that He has to say.

The hotter the fire, the deeper the lesson, the greater the maturity.

2. To Show Us Our Frailty

God knows how easily we can be fooled—by ourselves or others—into thinking that we're strong and can handle anything. But we aren't. Continuing in such an unhealthy delusion would be fatal to our lives. Discipline is God's way of saying, "It's pretty tough, isn't it? Need some help?"

It's not that we're strong and God tries to force us into being dependent on Him anyway. The reason He tries to show us our frailty is because we *are* frail. We're weak, puny, and ridiculously tiny compared to demons and the worst that life can throw against us. "Apart from me you can do nothing," He reminds us. "If you think you are standing firm, be careful that you don't fall!"[2]

Discipline comes to show us that we're clay, mere dust, and that we must hang on to God in order to live the Christian life.

Paul learned this lesson when he received a thorn in the flesh. What was this thorn? It was "a messenger of Satan, [sent] to torment me."[3] There are five billion people in this world and only so many demons. They can't be everywhere at once, and so they have to pick their targets. Paul was assigned a satanic messenger to torment him. With most of us, temptations come sporadically and with varying degrees of intensity. Paul was tempted all the time.

Paul pleaded with God three times to take the thorn away. I'm sure that his prayers arose from intense anguish and pain, and possibly went on for hours or days.

But God didn't take it away. He said, "My grace is sufficient for you, for my power is made perfect in weakness." Paul learned that his weakness and frailty would drive him to cling even more tightly to God, who would turn that weakness into strength—not just strength to resist the temptation, but a greater inner strength to be used as a reservoir in many future battles and projects.

It's a valuable thing to learn how frail, how really frail, we are. Only then are we finally willing—finally *able*—to run to God's lap and cry, "Save me, Papa!"

God won't let His strength compete with our false version of strength. Only when we're emptied of our own shoddy defenses can His strength come into our lives.

And then we can say with Paul, "Therefore I will boast all the more gladly about my weaknesses. . . . I *delight* [wild statement!] in weaknesses, in insults, in hardships, in persecutions, in difficulties." Because then, and only then, do we have available to us Christ's awesome power literally "spreading its tent" over us; only then are we really strong.

Years ago when I heard someone say, "I feel weak," the first thing I would tell him was that he could do whatever needed to be done, the "positive thinking" approach. Now when I hear someone say, "I feel weak," the first thing I say is, "Good! Now you're in a position to win."

Jesus Himself had to experience human weakness firsthand—in the desert . . . on the cross. "Because he himself *suffered* when he was tempted, he is able to help those who are being tempted."[4] He learned weakness by being weak, by becoming one of us. He knows just exactly how much help we need. How much can we accomplish with this kind of help?

"I can do *everything* through him who gives me strength."[5]

3. To Drive Out Unruliness and Bring Order into Our Lives

God is a God of order, and He wants us to be people of order. If we have unruliness in our lives, God will discipline us to drive it out.

What is unruliness? It's a sloppy life. It's an *undisciplined* life. The unruly person isn't involved in heinous sin; he's just careless with his ways. God encourages us to "be very careful, then, how you live."[6]

Marcie didn't keep very close track of her schedule. Her explanation was that she was "spontaneous" and didn't want to be too "tied down." She told herself that she could always remember the really important things. Then came the inevitable result: She missed a very important meeting. The consequences came in rapid succession: the terror at realizing she had forgotten the meeting; the "chewing out" she got from her boss in front of others; a negative performance review, which unfortunately was scheduled for the next week; and a smaller raise than she was expecting.

Was it sin to be careless? No. Was she trying to be rude? Probably not. But were there consequences? Yes. Our Father disciplines us to remove the unruliness and bring order into our lives.

Does this mean that God will "drop the hammer" on us for not keeping our calendar straight? No. He always fits the discipline to the need. Marcie's missed meeting was part of a long pattern. For many of us, the embarrassment of being late may be all the discipline that's necessary. If the underlying problem is deeper, He may let us miss a helpful conversation or lose a big sales order. But He'll do something to help us "throw off everything that hinders," including the things that are "permissible" but not "beneficial" or "constructive."

"The storm lasts until its mission is accomplished," said David Chilton. Jesus is in the business of taming stormy waves and turning them into glassy seas.

4. To Help Us Avoid Being Condemned with the World

One of the biggest problems we face is that we're closely connected with our evil sinful nature. In a sense, we're Siamese twins with that nature. Paul said, "When I want to do good, evil is right there with me."[7] We could say, "When I want to speak a word that will build up my child's heart, anger is right there with me." When we want to do good, evil *is* right there with us.

God wants to cut away things that "play into" the sinful nature. He'll bring pain into our lives, like a surgical knife, to separate us from that evil Siamese twin. Through suffering, we'll learn "not [to] live the rest of [our] earthly life for evil human desires, but rather for the will of God."[8] This doesn't mean, for example, that if we stub our toe we'll no longer have any wrong thoughts. But, if we'll respond to God's fire the right way, God will begin to clean the "evil human desires" out of our life and draw us closer to Himself.

Tim learned the truth of this Scripture in a deeper way when he injured his knee playing basketball. He hobbled around in a lot of pain for a couple of months, and when he finally went to the doctor, he learned that he needed surgery. So he went through the apprehension and the pain of the surgery and of the lengthy recuperation period that followed.

Throughout this entire time, Tim cried out to God for strength and help and insight into what was going on. He began asking God questions, studying sections of His Word, and drawing closer to Him in a way that he wouldn't have done if he hadn't had to suffer. Whenever a temptation came along, his response was, "Are you kidding? Do you think I'm going to sin against God now, right when I need His help to get through this excruciating trial? No way!" Tim discovered a rich meaning in the Scripture that tells us, "He who has suffered in his body is done with sin."[9]

Is Tim happy that he had to go through the physical and emotional pain of that trial? A few years ago, he would have said that he wasn't happy about the trial but that he could see how God had used it in his life. Now that he's learned to see God working behind the scenes, though, he can say, "Yes! I'm *glad* that God allowed my knee to be wrecked, because it pushed me away from the world and drew me so close to Him."

Suffering rightly taken and used can be a surprisingly useful tool to make the war against sinful desires easier.

5. To Bring Fire into Our Hearts

Jesus came to baptize His followers with a fire that would set their lives ablaze. He has at least three purposes for bringing this purifying fire of discipline into our hearts.

- God wants to *refine* us. "He will be like a refiner's fire or a launderer's soap. He will sit as a refiner and purifier of silver; he will purify the Levites and refine them like gold and silver. Then the LORD will have men who will bring offerings in righteousness, and the offerings of Judah and Jerusalem will be acceptable to the LORD, as in days gone by, as in former years."[10] The Lord wants to refine us so that our hearts will become pure fire and an acceptable offering to Him.

- God brings fire into our hearts to *test* us. "See, I have refined you, though not as silver; I have tested you in the furnace of affliction."[11] What kind of test is this? It's a test to see if we'll let Him do His work, let Him purify, let Him bring His eternal flame to life inside of us. He wants to see—and He wants us to know—what kind of people we really are. When everything is going well, it's easy to deceive ourselves into thinking that we're doing better than we really are. The furnace of affliction reveals our true character.

- God brings His fire into our hearts to *"salt"* us. *"Everyone"* will be salted with fire."[12] Everyone. Will the salting sting? Yes. Will it hurt? Yes. Then why does He do it? To bring out the real "flavor" He designed us to have. Many Christians talk about being "salt." But it's no ordinary salt, not just a granular salt. It's a salt of *fire*.

Shannon sat on the edge of her bed and felt the tears streaming down her cheeks. She crawled into the bed, pulled the covers over her head, and buried her face in the pillow. Her seven-year-old son, Adam, had just screamed at her that he hated her and wished she was dead. "Is *this* what it means to be a mother?" she sobbed out loud. She was hurt, frustrated, angry, and—it scared her to admit it—full of hate for this little boy who had once been inside her.

Then Shannon remembered a sermon about God's tendency to purify us and test us, and how He'll often do it in the closest of relationships and in the least expected of moments. "That's really an irritating tendency you have, God," she found herself saying. Then she laughed. "You *are* irritating, Lord," she said, remembering that our honest complaining to (not about) God won't shake Him off His throne. "Please help me see what's going on here," she prayed.

Over the next several days, truth began to flood her mind. Shannon realized that she had made Adam the center of her universe, building a demanding and arrogant spirit into him. She understood that she had become emotionally dependent on Adam, which made his opinion of her way too important and gave him the power to emotionally blackmail her. She knew she had failed this test of parenting. These thoughts stung her and made her cry again. But she purposed to get her relationship with her son back into balance and not let her own needs sidetrack her from the important mission God had given her.

It was said of Jesus, "Zeal for your house will consume me."[13] Like Shannon, when we've let God's fire burn in our hearts, destroying the chaff and purifying the rest, then His fire will flame out of us to affect those around us. It will ignite our lives and our goals and our directions, and God will be in everything in our lives.

We'll still have to wash dishes and go to work and put gas in the car, but everything we do will have God in the middle of it. It won't be God *and* our chores, but God *in* our chores—and in everything that we have and are and do.

6. To Help Us Develop Perseverance and Maturity

James says that we should consider trials pure joy because we *know* that the testing of our faith develops perseverance. Our sinful nature knows this—that's why it screams against trials. But if we're honest with ourselves, we know that we have to develop perseverance in order to become mature Christians.

How do trials accomplish such lofty goals? Trials shake us up. They knock us out of complacency and mediocrity. They force us to think about life in new ways. They require us to look deeper inside. They press us to draw on resources that have lain unused.

And they teach us tenacity. Tenacity, "the quality of holding fast," begins with patience: "Better [is] a patient man than a warrior."[14] This patience believes that truth and justice will *always* win out in the end, that wars will be won, that God will provide the wisdom and strength.

In the western classic *The Searchers*, two men are tracking a group of renegades who have kidnapped a female relative. After a long search covering many months, the younger man expresses his discouragement. The older man tells him that they *will* find her for a simple reason: the renegades don't understand that there's such a thing as a hunter who won't quit.

They search for *years,* far beyond what most of us are willing to do. And they finally find her and rescue her. It's a haunting story of incredible endurance and a refusal to quit in the midst of a trial. That's tenacity. That's perseverance.

Paul echoes James's wonderfully ridiculous "pure joy" idea: "We also *rejoice* in our sufferings, because we know that suffering produces perseverance."[15] The only way to rejoice in sufferings is to know that they are *useful.* They produce something, and that something is perseverance. The perseverance that comes from trials—the only true perseverance—sees the big picture when the "now" makes us scream; takes the long view when making it through today seems impossible; lives without fear when we can't stop trembling; and acts with confidence when there's no visible reason to do it.

If we persevere long enough, the trial produces maturity (strength and stability) and completeness (wholeness and integrity), or what Paul calls simply "character," the kind of character that's the real foundation for "hope."

I'd like to learn perseverance without enduring hardship. I'd like to become a mature Christian without trials. I'd like to have a complete life without suffering. I admit it.

I'd also like to eat fatty foods and not gain weight. I'd like to sleep only a little and not be fuzzy in my thinking. I'd like to never exercise and still stay in shape.

But things just don't work that way. I know people who have great goals but no perseverance. It saddens me to know that they won't accomplish very much, because it's perseverance, not good intentions, that achieves results.

The point to remember is that trials will come whether we learn from them or not. Will we feel the pain but miss the training?

Or will we use the pain to grow us strong?

7. So We Can Win Great Victories

There are no great victories without great battles. There's no great faith without great challenges. God gives us trials so that we can win great victories for His kingdom and have truly worthwhile things happen in our lives.

This is the spirit of Romans 8:37–39, where Paul, after talking about struggles and trials and challenges and disciplines, asks, "Can anything separate us from the love of God?" His answer is, "No!" He lists some very powerful enemies and obstacles but tells us that those things can't conquer us. Instead, they allow us to win great victories and to shout, "Hallelujah, God! *You* have done the work!"

First Kings 18 tells an awesome story of God's power. One prophet, Elijah, stood against 450 prophets of Baal in a great contest to see whether Baal or Almighty God would rain down fire from heaven and consume their sacrifices. Despite the pleas and frenzy of the false prophets, their god was silent—because he was no god at all. But when Elijah—a person "just like us"—prayed, God's fire fell from heaven and consumed not only the sacrifice but also the altar, the water around it, and even the soil it was sitting on. 450 to 1; 1 won.

This is the "incomparably great" power that we as Christians have in our arsenal. We have weapons in the right hand and the left, weapons that have "divine power to demolish strongholds."[16] We don't have to be afraid of God's enemies.

When the prophet Elisha awakened one morning to find the city surrounded with an army sent to capture *him*, he could have despaired like his servant did; perhaps many of us would too. Instead, he saw that God's horses and chariots of fire, sent to protect and deliver him, far outnumbered—and outpowered—those of the enemy army.

"Those who are with us are more than those who are with them," Elisha told his servant.[17] We don't ever need to lose. Not only do we have God on our side, but His angelic hosts outpower the demonic hosts and aren't dependent on our prayers for their strength.

Disciplines can seem so painful and unpleasant that we can easily forget how they lead to victories. But some of the greatest victories I've experienced have come when I was being disciplined by the Lord the hardest.

No great battles, no great victories.

8. So We Can Enter Fully into Christ's Experience

Jesus enters into our experience fully. He invites us as His friends, as His beloved, to enter fully into His.

Jesus allowed God to discipline Him, even though He Himself was the Son of God. He was God in the flesh, but He still endured many trials. People said cruel things about Him ("drunkard," "glutton," "blasphemer"), ran away from Him (James, John, the rich young ruler), and betrayed Him (Judas, Peter, us). His own family came to take Him away because they thought He was crazy. And finally, He endured the punishment of the cross, not to pay for His own sins (since He had none) but for ours.

Jesus suffered great trials, and one reason was to set an example for us. We shouldn't shirk or run away from discipline. Instead, we should follow in Jesus' steps and be glad in our spirits that God has brought discipline into our lives because it will make us finer, deeper, more chiseled people.

Why should we want to do this? "We share in his sufferings in order that we may *also* share in his glory."[18] Share in *Jesus'* glory? Stunning thought! These trials are making us more like Jesus and getting us ready for resurrection day. They are preparing us for the day when His glory is revealed—and ours along with it.

Jesus went through His most severe trials "for the joy set before him." What joy? The joy of completing the race, of winning a great victory, of showing others the way to life, of being able to say, "It is finished," of receiving recognition and rewards from God. We should do it for the same reasons. We "will not grow weary and lose heart" if we focus on the joy set before us. Jesus did it and won.

And so can we.

9. So We Will Long for a Better Country

Hebrews 11 recounts example after example of how God disciplined His children and how they, in turn, gave up their attachment to this world and learned to long for a better country. Trials help us to see how unsatisfying the world and its pleasures really can be and make us yearn for a place where "there will be no more death or mourning or crying or pain."[19]

God taught this lesson to His people in the desert. He let them experience hunger so that He could feed them and show them that "man does not live on bread alone but on every word that comes from the mouth of the LORD."[20] This trial was an invitation to lose their appetite for the pleasures of this world, which would never satisfy their hearts, and to hunger instead for relationship with God.

The trinkets can seem so important, can't they? The possessions, the perks, the holidays. But when trials come, they're a heavenly reminder that all is not well down here. "Don't get too comfortable," they say. "Don't confuse the moments that seem like heaven with heaven itself."

Does God want to bless us even now, while we're in the land and in mortal flesh? Absolutely. Is He ready to "graciously give us all things"? Yes, oh yes. Will He be "an ever-present help in trouble"?[21] Without question. Will He give us places of rest, still waters, and plateaus of peace even in this broken world? He promises it.

But is it also true that this is a thorny place, its beauty marred by sin and death? It is.

Trials, big and small, help us to remember.

10. To Bring Glory to God

John 9 records an encounter between Jesus and a man who had been born blind. As soon as they saw the blind man, the disciples asked Jesus, "Who sinned, this man or his parents?"

Now, what was wrong with their question? They were assuming that the blindness was a punishment. Assuming—drawing conclusions without information, knowledge, or wisdom—is one of the biggest diseases of life and Christianity. In a very real way, it is the deeper blindness.

Jesus said that the blindness wasn't a punishment. God had allowed the man to be born blind not to punish him, but because his healing would bring great glory to God.

When physical and emotional challenges come, God will use them to bring glory to Himself if we'll respond in the right way, if we'll "shine forth as gold."

As we've already seen, God also allows these trials to bring glory to *us* as well. "I consider that our present sufferings are not worth comparing with the glory that will be revealed in *us*," Paul said.[22] Glory is "praise, great renown, particular distinction, magnificence, splendor, sublime beauty." Suffering handled properly *always* leads to glory.

In fact, we're told that "our light and momentary troubles are achieving for us an eternal glory that far outweighs them all."[23] Troubles actually *earn* eternal glory. What an encouragement to persevere with a good attitude! And our troubles don't just earn "equivalent" glory, pound for pound.

An ounce of trouble gains a ton of glory.

Just as there was always a fire burning in the earthly temple, so the fire of the Holy Spirit is always burning in the temple of our bodies. That fire is continually testing the quality of our work and burning away impurities. It's giving us the chance to know here on this earth whether our efforts are resulting in things that will last for eternity—or in wood, hay, and straw, which will all burn up.

Someday we'll stand before the throne of God for the final testing of our works. If what we've built during our life survives the fire, we'll be rewarded and hear God say, "Well done, good and faithful servant." But if everything we've done is burned up, we'll suffer great loss. If we suffer well now, we won't have to suffer then.

What mercy God shows us by letting us know in this life the quality of the work we're producing. How heartbreaking it would be to have no clue before we got to the throne that all of our efforts had been in vain. When God sends fiery trials into our lives, He's testing us so that we can stop doing the things which won't last and start doing the things which will bring us blessing and rewards. Now.

And throughout eternity.

☋

SEVEN

*A man's own folly ruins his life, yet his heart rages
against the Lord.*
Proverbs 19:3

Seven Wrong Responses to Discipline

Pain is not evil, unless it conquer us.

Charles Kingsley

---

*I*n the last chapter, we looked at God's purposes for discipline. Now let's look at the "human" side of the equation, the very understandable but destructive and wrong responses to the refining fire of discipline.

There are at least seven wrong responses to discipline in our lives. The first one is an attempt to stop the pain at its source. The next three are internal efforts at dealing with the pain. The last three are external undertakings designed to push the pain off on God.

The common ingredient of all of these is that they seem to work for a while. But pain is like death: We know we'll die sooner or later, and all our struggles to change or deny that fact fall to the earth under the weight of an unchangeable reality. Pain, too, is a reality that must be faced. The wrong response to death brings more death—in this life and forever. The wrong response to pain brings more pain—more intense now and costly later on.

Let's look together at these ploys of sinful nature, the easy but devastatingly wrong answers to pain.

1. Ceasing to Live for God

The first wrong response is simply to stop growing, to stop doing whatever it is that's bringing the pain.

I had been involved as a pastor with an extended family that seemed to respond to my ministry. The husband and wife adopted me as a spiritual "father," even inviting me to come to a special school dinner in the role of "grandfather" to their children. The wife's sister, a woman with a shattered past, seemed to be coming back to life and sought my help on many occasions.

One evening, the three of them invited me home after church services were finished. I was tired and sick, but I thought it would be encouraging to them if I went.

When I got there, the wife wouldn't speak to me or even look at me. Her husband and sister sat down at the table with me. They were unable to control the wife or calm her down. Then they told me the reason for the invitation—they had concluded that I was a heretic because of the *translation* of the Bible that I used in preaching. Their father, it turned out, had taught them that all English translations other than the King James Version were evil, inspired by the devil, and probably written by communists or humanists.

Nothing would dissuade them. Out went all of the truth that they had learned, the love that we had shared. At one point, the sister showed me a list of denominations represented in the translation I used and said, "They even had *Anglicans* involved!" I pointed out that *everyone* involved in the King James translation was an Anglican, which slowed her down for a moment. (The irony of this accusation still intrigues me.)

The meeting went on and on. I felt sicker and sicker. By the time I got home, I was in total despair. I was ready to write off pastoring, church work, churches, Christians, people. Luther once told his congregation that he wasn't going to preach to them anymore because they "annoyed" him. I understood that feeling. I stayed in bed, locked in with the curtains drawn, for two days.

The temptation to stop my work was clear. It was so painful, and the results could at times seem so meager. People ignored truth, deserted their church "family," and returned evil for good. Why bother?

Because Jesus bothered. After three years of ministry, people who on Sunday shouted "Hosanna in the highest!" were by Thursday either silent or shouting "Crucify him!" One of His closest followers betrayed Him, and all the others deserted Him—Peter alone followed at a distance but eventually denied Him. Only John and a few women made their way to the cross. Only three women made it to the grave on resurrection day. Most people quit.

By God's grace, strength, and help, we don't need to succumb to the temptation to quit. If we don't, the pain will produce a deeper life, love, and ministry.

And people a little more refined by the Master.

2. Avoiding and Denying Pain

Pain avoidance starts in childhood. It's very effective at the physical level. If a child puts his hand on a hot stove, he learns not to do that again. If he touches a socket and gets shocked, he probably won't touch it again.

But we can learn to avoid pain so well that we throw the proverbial baby out with the bath water. We can learn not to touch hot stoves, but also not to touch hot spirituality; not to put our fingers in the socket, but also not to connect with *the* Socket, Christ. We can run from God's fire rather than letting it burn in our hearts.

Pain avoidance can be deadly, especially in the spiritual realm. We can refuse to let God's Word burn into our lives and help us face the reality of who we are, and how we came to be that way, and how our lives might be negatively impacting those around us—because facing the truth can hurt.

Denial, on the other hand, can seem peaceful—at first. Denial at the start says that there is no pain; then it tells us that the pain isn't serious. Finally, it persuades us that there's just no reason for the pain. It uses pretending as an anesthetic. It can seem much easier to go through life avoiding the real issues in our hearts and in our families, blaming, instead, all our conflicts and our inner turmoil on someone or something else.

But eventually we won't be able to pretend anymore. The results will show.

Tom was a workaholic, finding his meaning and identity in his career. After his daughter was born, he was assigned a huge project. He came home after she was asleep and left before she was awake. For six months he hardly saw her or held her at all. The pain of discipline came when she cried every time he took her in his arms.

Tom grieved deeply and cried tears of change and growth. Although he hadn't sinned, he was taught by discipline how he could do better. He re-sorted his priorities and placed more emphasis on relationships and less on career. He decided to accept less in the way of pay and promotions to get more things money just can't buy. He found satisfaction in a good connection with his daughter that he had always assumed could only be found in meaningful work.

Tom could have responded very differently. He might have sunk into a self-pitying depression. Or he could have blamed his problems on an unreasonable boss or a harsh economy or an ungrateful child or a wife who wasn't doing enough to help out. He could have spent even more time at work and less at home in order to avoid the pain all together. By responding in these ways, Tom would have avoided facing the real source of the pain—the fact that he was a workaholic—and would have missed the whole value of the discipline.

Jonah made this mistake. When he was told to go preach in Ninevah, he ran away from God instead.

Jonah had a test. He was told to go preach to a hard-hearted bunch that probably wouldn't listen. Anyone who has ever tried to share truth with others can understand why Jonah would want to avoid the whole thing and go a different direction.

Abraham, on the other hand, didn't try to avoid pain. When he was told to sacrifice his son—a son for whom he had waited years and years—he got up *early* and got on with the discipline. He knew he had a tough assignment (to put it mildly) but that it was *not* punishment. He knew that he and his son *would* come back down the hill (he says so to his servants) because he'd concluded that God would raise Isaac from the dead right on the spot. This incredible faith, this running *to* a trial rather than away, is why Abraham is the father of all who believe.

And why Jonah isn't.

3. Growing Weary and Losing Heart

We've already looked at how pain is used by God to help us "throw off" hindrances, but a common and powerful temptation we face when pain comes into our lives is to consider *it* the hindrance.

Someone once said that hindrances are those fearful things that show up as obstacles on our path when we take our eyes off the goal. If we stop looking at Christ, and "well done, good and faithful servant," and the eternal rewards—if, in other words, we forget about heaven—the trials that come along will swallow us up. We'll find ourselves asking, "Where's God? Why has He forsaken me?" We *can* forget the joy at the end of the trial and grow weary and lose heart.

In so many ways, life is short. In one critical area, however, it's fearfully long. Insults and hardships and persecutions and difficulties, accumulated over years, can bend and break our hearts. The load can come to a point where we feel as though we have no heart left, as though our heart—our ability to go on with life—is gone.

What are the thoughts that tell us we're in danger of going under? "Evil is just too strong." "People are not worth the effort." "Can I really trust God again?" "I feel like I'm hoping in vain." "I used to have such confidence in God."

We can be weighted down by the trials of others as well. This is why Paul told people not to be discouraged by his sufferings. We can find ourselves saying, "If that could happen to her, then what's the point?"

The point is not to grow weary and lose heart. We can draw on God's wisdom to see the meaning and value of discipline, and Christ's strength to endure and win. We can understand how the very length of the trial is part of the test, and we can refuse to buckle under the weight that—at the moment—seems to have no end. But it *does* have an end. Winter, in God's creation, is always followed by spring. The trial *will* end. The only question is, will *we* come to an end before the trial does?

May it never be.

4. Numbing the Pain

Much of modern life is designed to numb the pain of living.

Medical science has produced some marvelous medications for reducing or eliminating pain. For that, we can all be grateful. Physical pain can reduce us to tears, to whimpering, to screaming, even to unconsciousness.

I once had a tooth that was dying. I somehow got to the dentist, even though I could hardly think because of the inconceivable pain. The dentist made an appointment with an oral surgeon for several hours later. He must have noticed the look on my face when he told me about the delay because he offered me a shot to numb the throbbing until I could get to more permanent help. Although his prices weren't cheap, he didn't charge me one-tenth of what I would have been willing to pay for that shot.

The pain itself, however, wasn't the enemy. It was really a friend, telling me that something was very, very wrong with my mouth. But it *seemed* like the enemy. That's the way it usually is. Pain that warns and guides us seems like the enemy, while the real enemy—the dying roots, the diseased organs, the cancerous tissues—lie just out of sight.

If we don't pay attention to physical pain, we can get sicker and sicker. We can die. If I had gone from dentist to dentist and gotten numbing after numbing, I would have felt relatively "fine." Eventually, though, my mouth would have been too sore and bruised to take any more shots, and the real problem would have led to other difficulties far beyond itself.

The lesson is true for our spiritual lives. Pain is there to tell us that something is just not right. God is gracious and allows some anesthetic—sleep, an encouraging word, a lovely fall day, a small act of kindness by someone we love. We can and should welcome the relief. We know, if we're seeing clearly, that the time will come when the source of the pain will be taken away or transformed by God.

The danger comes when we decide to go after so much anesthetic that we don't have to understand the value of the pain or ever face its source.

This is where the world comes in. It has a cornucopia of apparently delightful agents to deaden the unwanted pain. From things not evil in themselves—television, movies, music, sports, parties, food, books, involvement in "issues"—to stronger "medications"—lust, anger, greed, gossip, slander, jealousy, ambition. There is something for every occasion. Even actual medications—alcohol, prescription drugs, illegal drugs—can be used to numb spiritual pain.

But they don't fix the problem. This is the approach that curses the thermometer for recording a fever, that adjusts a pressure gauge rather than reducing a dangerously high pressure level in a mechanical system. The pain is there to show us our need, but we bury it.

The time will come, though, when the unfaced pain will have the last word, when the thing we needed to face, but didn't, buries us instead.

5. Making Excuses for God

So much of the teaching on discipline and punishment takes the form of making excuses for God.

A typical version goes like this: A barrage of examples is given to show that life is tough, that Christians can't expect to be delivered from their trials, and that it's not reasonable to expect to understand what God is doing. Next, it's stated piously that God is "sovereign"—which He is, but which isn't relevant to the point.

Saying "God is sovereign" seems to honor to God, but in this application it isn't. Why not? Because of what's behind the statement. The underlying implication is either that God isn't really a *good* Father (at least not "good" in a way that we can understand) or that His will isn't "good, pleasing, and perfect," but rather something—often terrible—to which we must resign ourselves. In one of its worst forms, it implies that God may have good intentions, but He really isn't in control.

In fact, saying, "Oh well, it was God's will," keeps us from having to think, to feel pain, to look realistically at what we're doing that might be continuing or increasing the pain. And even though our comments sound pious, they don't keep us from the negative results of hidden bitterness against God and of refusing to face what we need to change. Ironically, making excuses for God will eventually separate us in our hearts from Abba.

God needs no excuses—certainly not from His creatures. God doesn't need us to make excuses for Him, and He doesn't make excuses for Himself. God could defend Himself, but He chooses not to do so. He wants us to look at life from His perspective rather than through a flawed human view. He expects us to understand that He *always* has a purpose—a good purpose—for His discipline.

And that He always makes sense.

6. Grumbling and Complaining

As we begin to face hardships and trials and pain, if we *gripe* about them, God's anger will be aroused.

When the knife comes to circumcise the excess flesh from our hearts, when the fire comes to burn the underbrush out of our hearts, God wants us to yield to Him and say, "Father, it hurts. It's painful. But please take it all. Burn it all. Cut it all out of my heart. I don't want any more illusions. I don't want any more false peace. And so when it hurts, I'll cling to You until Your work is finished."

This was Job's smashing victory: "Though he slay me, yet will I hope in Him" (Job 13:15).

We're warned severely: "Do not grumble, as some of them did—and were killed by the destroying angel."[1] The "some of them" were *God's people* in the desert. They were grumbling about their trials. After enough grumbling, the result was terrible: The trial became a maximum punishment. The people were killed by an angel.

A pretty sobering thought.

7. Blaming God

After excusing God and griping about God, we can come to the logical but atrocious conclusion of blaming God. This is an all-too-common occurrence in Christianity—in *humanity*. We can refuse to listen to His answers about our complaints *to* Him, then in our bitterness ignore what He's saying to us related to our complaints *about* Him, and finally just wallow in our bitterness against Him.

But this is folly. "A man's own folly ruins his life, yet his heart rages against the LORD."[2] As the discipline turns to punishment, as our rage crescendos, as our lives ebb away in our hardheartedness, we end our lives in a black hole. The abyss of despair always comes from laying blame at God's holy feet.

This was Job's smashing failure: "Who is this that darkens my counsel with words without knowledge?" (Job 38:2).

May it never be.

———

As with most of life, there's only one right way to respond to discipline, but many wrong ways. With God's help, we don't ever need to respond wrongly again.

The consequences, which we'll look at in the next chapter, are just too great.

You will say, "How I hated discipline! How my heart spurned correction! I have come to the brink of utter ruin in the midst of the whole assembly."
Proverbs 5:12, 14

Four Consequences of Responding Wrongly to Discipline

[He] was rich in the . . . capacity to learn nothing and forget nothing.

Barbara Tuchman

---

*O*ne of the great things about our God—and one of the most sobering—is that He won't *make* us respond properly to the formative pain that comes into our life.

His refusal to force us into growth is steadfast. He simply won't do it. He won't make us "be good." He provides the pain—the disciplines, the trials, the spirit-stretching experiences—and the wisdom and strength to handle them, but He never makes us react in the way that's best for our future. He leaves the choice squarely with us. It's quite a statement of how much He respects us, the dignity He offers us that imperfect people often will not.

We've just finished looking at the wrong responses to pain. There are many ways to be wrong if that's where our heart is heading. In this chapter, we'll look at the "down side" of responding in one of those ways to the developmental plan of God for our lives. The consequences are devastating and remind us that as good as it can be for us when we struggle through to the right answer, it can be just as bad when we miss the point.

1. We Will Get Sterner Discipline

"Stern discipline awaits him who leaves the path" (Prov. 15:10). The path of life is found by only a few. Because it's narrow, we can all too easily wander off of it. Although we can't lose our position in Christ, we can lose our balance (as well as blessings in this life and the life to come). This is why we're told to "Make level paths for your feet."[1]

God has a disciplinary plan of action for our lives to help us run faster and better. If we miss it and instead begin wandering off the path, He has to "step up" the heat. His discipline becomes more strict, more severe, more intense. He wants us to realize that we're not running our race to win and that we're no longer in contention for "the prize."

Stern discipline is different from discipline. All of us who belong to God undergo discipline because we're His sons and daughters. The only way to avoid discipline is to be "illegitimate," meaning we're not really a child of God. Those who reject God as their Father *can* receive discipline, and *will* receive some, because God is gracious and *wants* them to be His children. But they won't be disciplined fully and in an ongoing manner, for they're not true children. What they're asking for is punishment, not discipline. God's discipline of His children, on the other hand, is both persistent and non-optional.

Stern discipline, however, is "voluntary." We don't have to receive this kind of discipline. It's the kind that only comes when we respond wrongly to God's fatherly discipline. We "invite" this kind of discipline by our own wooden-headedness and wooden-heartedness.

Breanna had always been a very open person. After she became a Christian, she shared her heart openly with anyone who claimed to be a Christian. She was vulnerable about the details of her life, since she assumed that these people would be trustworthy secret-keepers. The discipline to correct her poor discernment began when some Christians withdrew from her because they didn't like what she shared or because it made them feel uncomfortable. Others used her sharing as a source for gossip.

But Breanna persisted in sharing with people who weren't deeply committed to her life. She continued to cast her "pearls" (her "heart treasures") before those who trampled them and then tore her to pieces. She shared confidentially with Jocelyn some of the problems in her troubled marriage. Jocelyn broke the confidence. This started a chain of events that ended with a legal attack by Breanna's husband over child custody.

It was stern discipline indeed. But Breanna finally heeded the message and learned discernment. This new discernment left her better loved, as she learned to spend her energies on "receiver/givers" rather than "taker/users." It also gave her strong boundaries and left her better protected, as she wisely kept wolves and relational game-players at a distance.

God sends stern discipline when, by our sickly actions, we've shown that we need stronger medicine. It, too, comes from a loving Father, who is very, very concerned. Our desire to avoid this kind of discipline should be even stronger than our desire to live an "easy" life or to keep doing things the same old way. The price is just too high. This is why we're told that "he who hates correction is stupid."[2]

Father, help us not to invite Your stern discipline.

2. We Will Come to Poverty and Shame

"He who ignores discipline comes to poverty and shame" (Prov. 13:18). In this simple sentence, God tells us that if we ignore discipline—even stern discipline—we can end up in two desperate conditions.

The first is poverty. Poverty can include financial poverty, for certainly an undisciplined life can be unproductive and wasteful. But it can involve more: spiritual poverty, emotional poverty, relational poverty. At its worst, it includes the poverty of "hope deferred, [which] makes the heart sick," because only "the desires of the *diligent* are fully satisfied."[3]

The second condition is shame. Shame is "a painful emotion aroused by the recognition that one has failed to act, behave, or think in accordance with the standards which one accepts as good." Legitimate shame always comes after the fact—when the discipline has been ignored, warning signs have been passed, and sloppy living has won the day. There is illegitimate shame, in which our consciences have been trained by erroneous beliefs or rigid relational or behavioral control. This kind of shame should be rejected. But the result of ignoring discipline is legitimate shame, in which we know we're not living up to God's expectations.

This is where it's so easy for us to miss the point. God has been trying to speak to us, and we've ignored Him. Now the pain increases, going past stern discipline and on to real poverty and shame. In part this is a consequence, and in part this is God's provision of another opportunity to come to our senses and respond rightly to the discipline. But we can miss it and try to convince ourselves that somehow we're "suffering for Jesus."

Margaret was living an embarrassing life. Her care for herself—clothing, hygiene, relationships—was almost nonexistent, while in a bizarre way her self-centeredness was all-consuming. She moved from church to church, continually draining their "help the poor" resources. She claimed she had been fired from many jobs "for being a Christian."

But Margaret was living a totally undisciplined life. She wasn't doing what she could do. She lost her jobs because she spent the whole day talking about God instead of doing her work for Him. She had ignored much discipline—not having enough money to pay her bills, not having enough food, admonition from those she'd taken advantage of, and even stern discipline—rotting teeth, a terrible reputation, a deteriorating sanity. The result of her entrenched refusal to listen was entrenched poverty and shame. There are those who are legitimately poor or unjustly shamed. Margaret wasn't one of them.

We can end up deeply ashamed of ourselves. "He who ignores discipline despises himself."[4] To despise is "to look down upon, to feel contempt for." The worst poverty isn't the financial kind; it's the emptiness of a bankrupt soul. The worst shame isn't the kind heaped on us by others; it's the conviction within us that at first whispers, and later shouts, "You wasted your life."

A lot of Christian suffering isn't suffering for Jesus, although this is what we would like to believe. It's just suffering—brought on by our own disregard of discipline, a consequence of our own stony-heartedness. We can put on a martyr's face, but if the fault is our own, we'll be swamped with ever-increasing poverty and shame.

And sadly, we'll earn nothing from our pain.

3. We Will Lead Others Astray

"He who heeds discipline shows the way to life, but whoever ignores correction leads others astray."[5]

This is a powerful statement about the impact that our response to discipline has on others. If we "heed" discipline—pay attention to it, learn from it, change, grow—others will see it and know how to find life. What an encouragement to us who are parents! If we respond properly to discipline, we can have the assurance that our children will actually be able to see the way to life clearly.

But everything in life has a balancing truth. This passage tells us that ignoring correction will not only harm us, but will harm others as well. They'll see us going our own undisciplined way, and they'll be encouraged to follow us in our wandering. If we're sloppy in our thoughts and words and habits, they will be too.

Sam was always in a hurry and seemed to enjoy speeding in his car. His impatience with everyone on the road—a classic and dangerous way to release tension and frustration—was legendary. The discipline of several tickets and near mishaps didn't slow him down at all. Although he lectured his son Tom on the need to be a careful driver, the power of example spoke much louder. Tom became a speeder, also ignoring disciplines along the way. Sam's refusing to heed discipline was an unseen explanation for Tom's involvement in a number of serious accidents.

If we won't let God's disciplinary fire have its way in our soul, if we refuse to face the fire in the undeveloped or misguided areas of our life, then a different kind of fire will come out of us and burn the loved ones around us. In fact, the term "loved ones" isn't completely accurate here. If we're burning them up, we aren't really loving them. We're showing them how to be a wildfire.

If we wonder why those around us seem so undisciplined, perhaps we don't need to analyze them first.

A mirror may do very nicely.

4. We Will Die

This result is stunning: We can die due to lack of discipline (Prov. 5:23).

What does it mean to "die for lack of discipline"? It means just that: death. There's no neutral in the Christian life, or in any life. We're either moving toward God and blessing, or away from God to cursing. We're either for Christ or against Him. We're either growing or shriveling, living or dying.

We don't like this idea. It isn't comfortable. It doesn't fit with our idea of a "loving" God, or of "grace," or of "finding a middle ground." Would God let us die just because we lack discipline? Yes. If we're "led astray by [our] own great folly"—which is where we'll always end up if we ignore His loving discipline—then God will let our life ebb away.

There are many ways to be dead. We can be spiritually dead, mentally dead, emotionally dead, volitionally dead, and, of course, physically dead. Physical death may not even be the worst of the list. Those who commit suicide are saying that physical death is *not* as bad as the others—and that it seems to them (however erroneously) to be a release from the other "deaths" they're experiencing.

Creighton was one under God's discipline who came to such death. God would speak to him from His Word about an issue, and Creighton at times would even get excited. But like a rootless plant in the hot sun he would soon give it up and fade away. He resented criticism, no matter how gently it was given, and said that even a teacher in elementary school had told him he was too defensive and unwilling to be disciplined, trained, and corrected.

There was an apparent softness to this man at first. But year by year, inch by inch, his heart turned to cold, hard rock as he ignored and rejected discipline from God. He became critical of others. He would spend his time in Bible studies looking up Scriptures to refute whatever the teacher was saying. He became jealous. He began undercutting authority and attacking people behind their backs.

"What has happened to all your joy?" was a fitting question for Creighton.[6] He *had* seemed to have a genuineness, a joy, about him earlier. But it all disappeared into the dust—first to spiritual and emotional poverty, then to shame as his icy heart became known by the people around him, and finally to the death of his inner life and joy. The last time I saw him was when he stormed out of a meeting in which I was urging him to reconcile with someone he had wounded severely. He was still breathing.

But on the inside he was very, very dead.

It's the easiest thing in the world to resent and try to resist God's discipline. It's unpleasant. It's painful. It presses for change and growth.

But the really glorious truth is that despite the seemingly unbearable pressure, we don't need to respond wrongly. We can choose to listen to discipline and be honored.

Peter gives us a great reminder: "Dear friends, do not be surprised at the painful trial you are suffering, as though something strange were happening to you."[7] We *can* be surprised by trials. If we've lived very long we probably shouldn't be, but if we aren't careful we can be caught off guard. Peter tells us more: We shouldn't think this "trial" business is strange. It goes with the turf. It's part of living. And we don't have to respond wrongly to discipline because we have the best helper that money can't buy.

"In this world you *will* have trouble," the Master told us, "but take heart! I have overcome the world."[8]

Take heart, friend.

NINE

Then Jesus told his disciples a parable to show them that they
should always pray and not give up.
Luke 18:1

The Right Response to Discipline

As sure as ever God puts His children in the furnace,
He will be in the furnace with them.

Charles Spurgeon

*D*iscipline is a test of faith.

In some ways it's the ultimate test because "no discipline seems pleasant at the time, but painful."[1] It's so hard for it to sink in: *Discipline never ever seems pleasant at the time.* If it didn't challenge us and make us uncomfortable, it wouldn't be discipline. We'd like our discipline to come sugarcoated, but true discipline is never soft and easy—and it never leaves us weak and flabby.

In fact, discipline is *always painful.* There is no other kind of discipline. Being a follower of Jesus is a joyful experience, but it's also a painful one. If we follow Him, there are times when we won't have a place to lay our head, times when we'll be treated very badly, times when the going will get rough and we'll be tempted to turn back. "Can you drink the cup I am going to drink?" He asks us. "If anyone would come after me he must . . . take up his cross."[2] Discipline can be tough—very tough.

Discipline doesn't seem pleasant *at the time,* which implies two things. First, we'll initially have to see the long-term pleasantness of discipline with the eyes of faith, "being sure of what we hope for and certain of what we do not see."[3] Second, a time will come when we *will* see the pleasantness of discipline with our own eyes.

When will that be? "Later on, however, it produces a harvest of righteousness and *peace* for those who have been trained by it." It produces righteousness, because "God disciplines us for our good, that we may share in his holiness."[4] It produces peace, because discipline tames the heart and eliminates internal division and strife, the opponents of peace. When we finally experience righteousness and peace, the discipline will seem pleasant indeed.

Martha was a single mother with two children who were rebellious. Every day was a trial, many days a war. The children complained constantly, resisted her authority, and always seemed to be in trouble. She gradually saw how the children's father had contributed to this painful problem through his disrespect of her in front of the children and his swings between anger and indulgence. Then God began to show her—painfully—how her own actions were contributing to the situation. She was excusing bad behavior ("It's because she was sick/tired/hurt"), giving in to emotional blackmail ("I don't love you, Mommy"), and complaining about many things in the children's hearing.

The pain of dealing with real, live rebels blew away her erroneous parenting "theories" and exposed the weaknesses of her own heart. Martha listened. She grew to understand that her primary role was not to be a caretaker with a list of rules, but to be a complete woman with a heart of both compassion and convictions. She began to search her children's hearts through prayer and conversation and to lead by a better example through stopping her own complaining. As her own heart was quieted, she was better able to tame the wild passions of her two children.

Discipline brought Martha a greater measure of righteousness and peace, but only because she was willing to be trained by it. We can face discipline, which is always unpleasant at the time, and refuse to be trained by it. We still feel all of the pain, but we don't receive any of the benefit.

Instead of righteousness and peace, it can produce rage and pandemonium.

How, then, are we trained by God's discipline? By persisting. Persisting in what? In our faith, in our attitude, and in our work.

We are trained by persisting in our faith because we're to "believe that he exists and that he rewards those who *earnestly* seek him."[5] We don't doubt His character. We trust in His deliverance. We purpose to "be joyful *always,* pray *continually,* [and] give thanks in *all* circumstances."[6] This is God's will for us. He wants us to see His hand so clearly in the hardship that rejoicing, praying, and thanking become as much a part of our being as breathing.

We are trained by persisting in our attitude because our attitude is the overflow of our heart. It will either say, "Though he slay me, yet will I hope in him" or "Curse God and die!"[7] This doesn't mean that we can't complain to God; the Scriptures are full of complaints from godly people to their God. God knows how tough life is and understands—even expects—our "letting it all out" to Him.

What we can't do is complain *about* God, which shows an alienated heart and brings His judgment. "Do *everything* without complaining."[8] Why? Surely God isn't *that* tough on complaining? "And do not grumble, as some of them did—*and were killed by the destroying angel*."[9] The Israelites were in a desert, did the "understandable" thing and complained, and had a terrible encounter with an angel whose job description should make us want to avoid him. Complain *to* God, yes; complain *about* God, never!

We are trained by persisting in our work because we're encouraged not to "become weary in doing good." Why not? "For at the proper time we *will* reap a harvest *if* we do not give up."[10] It's the "giving up" that kills us, that wrecks the training, that destroys the harvest. From beginning to end, we're encouraged to continue in the face of even seemingly overwhelming trials.

God knows that persevering is hard. So He tells us to "strengthen your feeble arms and weak knees [and to] 'make level paths for your feet.'"[11] He tells us to go "into strict training," to beat our bodies into submission.[12] He exhorts us to "endure hardship . . . like a good soldier."[13] He warns us to "watch out that you do not lose what you have worked for, but that you may be rewarded fully."[14]

This "persisting" is serious business. God is trying to teach us, to train us, to make us mature and complete, to give us righteousness and peace. He has a plan for doing it which includes unpleasant-at-the-time discipline. Will we learn? Will we be trained? Will we become mature and complete, not lacking anything? Will we have righteousness and peace?

Or will we give up?

Throw Off the Belief Hindrances

Eleanore was taught that she must submit to her husband without question, "perform" for him in their physical relationship, and make child rearing the whole of her life. Her husband has taken advantage of these beliefs to control her, to get her to do things that violated her conscience (not to mention her sense of being loved and respected), and to isolate her and greatly reduce her ability to use her gifts and talents.

Eleanore feels a desperate pain. She has a vague but pressing sense of loneliness, even alienation. She fights against resentment toward her husband, but feels guilty for even having to fight the negative feelings. The moments when she feels satisfied with raising her children seem fewer and fewer. She feels that she's had to die to her hunger for life and love.

Eleanore has had to create a "value" system to hold these beliefs that have no basis in the Bible, beliefs that are killing her heart. Biblical authority has the exalting heart of a servant, not the controlling heart of a tyrant. Her life belongs to God—she's been bought with a price—and has a dignity that no one has the right to transgress. And while mothering is a noble activity, a woman is a multitalented being whose life and ministries should be expanded, not contracted. The "Proverbs 31 woman" mothers effectively by letting her children see her live a full life, not by making them the center of her universe.

All of us, like Eleanore have rough edges to our lives. God wants to smooth these edges, to make us finished sculptures which show forth our unique version of His image. To do this, He has to hammer and chisel and scrape—none of which is easy or painless but which must be done. All of the "excess baggage" must go.

Hebrews 12:1 says, "Let us throw off everything that hinders." All of us have baggage, weights, and chains on us. These are old beliefs and ways of thinking and saying and approaching things—the "empty way of life handed down to [us] from [our] forefathers."[15] We have to shed these bogus beliefs if we want to run an effective, unhindered race. How do we do this?

- *Meditate.* We can "get quiet" before God and ask Him to show us the hindrances, whether they're opinions, relationships, circumstances, or habits. We can purpose not to "dodge" anything He tells us.

- *List.* We can make a list of the things we don't like about ourselves, our lives, and our ways. We can put everything down, regardless of where the feeling comes from or whether it's really a problem. This is the time for total honesty.

- *Review.* We can take our list and search the Bible for insight on the items, one by one. We can write down the references and go back to them over the next several days.

- *Prioritize.* After we've thought about our list and reviewed it under God's guiding hand, we can put the list in priority order, based on the things that are causing us the greatest harm. This isn't an exact science, so we don't have to be too concerned that we might not get it "right."

- *Study.* We can take the first item and seek out resources—commentaries, books, tapes, magazines, pamphlets, novels—which can give us more insight. We shouldn't be afraid to take whatever time is necessary. It took a long time to accumulate these weights. If we'll commit to the effort, we can throw them off.

- *Write.* We can get a notebook, list the first item and our "findings," and then move on to the next item and do the same. We can write things down as we see them and not try to "pretty it up." We can list the consequences—the pain—we see at work to wake us up. We should leave some room to add—perhaps in a different color—the specific ways we need to change.

- *Share.* We can take our prioritized lists and our notebooks to an intimate, trusted friend and share what we've learned. We can ask him or her to be honest with us about blind spots: things we've left off the list, our prioritization, our scriptural and other research, our planned changes.

It is critical that we do the first six steps before we begin sharing with others. We'll be tempted to skip our private work because it's hard. It can seem much easier to just ask someone, but our questions will be incomplete and shallow—and even close friends won't see or tell us about everything. We have to break up the unplowed ground before we ask others to plant seeds.

We can also carry the weight of sins committed against us with which we have never dealt and the old ways of reacting which we learned because of those offenses. The damaging beliefs can range from telling ourselves we weren't really harmed to trying to convince ourselves that those unresolved issues won't control our lives in the future. We can follow the steps above to get a "handle" on these broken areas. If the wounds are very deep, we may need to seek help from experienced counselors.

Throw Off the Behavior Hindrances

"'Everything is permissible for me' [not speaking of sin, of course], but not everything is beneficial."[16] Is it permissible for an endurance runner to sit around and eat nothing but chocolate cake all day long? Of course. But if he does, he won't win any marathons. He probably won't even finish the race. Eating only chocolate cake is permissible, but it's not beneficial. There are weights in our lives which aren't sins but which also aren't helpful.

A common weight today is the "alpha-wave" syndrome. Did you know that a television's patterns can actually anesthetize our brains? We can be watching it without our thought processes ever working! It's like being immobilized. Some have concluded that we have less brain activity when we're watching television than when we're doing nothing!

Is television sinful in and of itself? No. It's simply a technology that allows us to see things that people in past generations never even heard of, much less imagined or saw. It can have real value. But can it become something that hinders? Yes.

Suppose that we watch only good programs without any "trash," but we do it eight hours a day for the rest of our lives. What will be the result? We'll be much less than God intended us to be because we could have spent that time learning and doing things that had more value. We can miss running the race laid out for us because we have the weight of television hanging onto us. We can watch life instead of living it.

In order to run our race, we're going to have to throw off all the weights we carry. They won't fall off instantly when we become Christians, or when we first become aware of the weights, or when we pray about them. We have to make a conscious effort to discard these life-killing burdens. It's more like taking off twenty pounds than taking off a back pack.

God's Device for Eliminating Hindrances

How do we throw off the things that hinder us? That comes through the pain—sometimes excruciating pain—of discipline. God is going to bring trials into our lives to help us throw off those weights.

The proper response to the pain of discipline is *not* to stop running or to turn around and head in another direction. Instead, it's to throw off those weights as we run so that we can run a more effective race—faster, straighter, smoother.

The only way we're going to be able to keep going in the midst of great pain is if we can see the hand of God in the middle of our circumstances. If we use our circumstances as a reason to question whether or not God cares about us, or even exists at all, then we'll grow weary and lose heart and stop running. But if we, through faith, see the hand of God—

even in the darkness—we'll come through the pain stronger, more honed, more mature, and more energized.

The birth of my youngest daughter was a dark time of trials. Pam went into premature labor at twenty weeks. Through God's great power and the knowledge He has given the medical community, the birth was delayed until twenty-nine weeks. The months of torturous trial seemed to end with the birth of a three-pound, ten-ounce gift from heaven.

Bethany started the day—started her life in the world of air—breathing on her own. But by afternoon the picture changed. She was given morphine to allow a breathing tube to be put in place. She had an allergic reaction to the morphine, and her body shut down. I stood watching helplessly through the window in intensive care as an alert sounded, and doctors and nurses crowded around her little plastic bin.

The raging voices of death and destruction screamed at me. "It's over! What a fool you were to trust God!" I was scared to death—about death. In the next few minutes, the words of Hebrews 10:35–39 became a living reality in my life: "So do not throw away your confidence; it will be richly rewarded. You need to persevere so that when you have done the will of God, you will receive what he has promised. For in just a very little while, 'He who is coming will come and will not delay. But my righteous one will live by faith. And if he shrinks back, I will not be pleased with him.' But we are not of those who shrink back and are destroyed, but of those who believe and are saved."

The choice was clear: throw away my confidence, shrink back, and be destroyed; or persevere, live by faith, and receive what He has promised. It wasn't a question of willpower. It was a question of walking by edifying faith or by terrifying sight. It was a matter of knowing that Jesus went through black trials and so He knows how to help us through them too. It wasn't a complex issue of theology but rather a child-like run into the arms of Abba God.

The little girl lived. Six weeks of intensive care followed. She came home with a heart monitor and an oxygen tank. As I write this, Bethany is a robust, healthy second-grader who loves to read and ride her bike.

God insists on using on-the-job training (trials) along with classroom instruction (Bible study) to improve us. We long for the cheap, sacrifice-free education.

But He just won't give it to us.

How Long, O Lord? And How Tough?

All trials aren't the same in kind and degree. Every day we face battles: rude comments from others, disobedient children, too much to do. Here and there in a lifetime we come face-to-face with all-out war.

The psalmist knew this. Psalm 44 records the honest lament of his heart as he faced one of those major life trials. He knew how great God was, and he remembered how well God had taken care of His people in the past.

But suddenly that care and protection seemed to have disappeared, and God's people were being "devoured" and "crushed." They were "a haunt for jackals" and were "covered . . . with deep darkness." Those are strong words—very strong words. A jackal is an awful, scroungy animal that steals carcasses from other predators. To feel as though jackals are prowling and howling around us is to feel crushed and nearly dead.

Had God's people sinned? Were they being punished for disobeying His law? The psalmist's answer is an emphatic "No." "All this happened to us, though we had *not* forgotten you or been false to your covenant. Our hearts had *not* turned back; our feet had *not* strayed from your path" (emphasis added).

So what conclusion does he draw? Does he say, "God must not care about me" or "Maybe there isn't a God"? No! He says, in effect, "God, you cared for me and gave me victory. Then it got really tough, God, and I don't understand why at this moment because I haven't sinned. It can't be punishment—but it's a discipline a hundred times bigger than me." Then, with his confidence in God filling his heart, he says, "For your sake we face death all day long; [for your sake] we are considered as sheep to be slaughtered." No trial was going to drive him away from God.

Paul understood this when he wrote in Romans 8:35–37, "Who shall separate us from the love of Christ? Shall trouble or hardship or persecution or famine or nakedness or danger or sword?" To answer his question, Paul quotes the psalm above: "'For your sake we face death all day long; we are considered as sheep to be slaughtered.'"

In other words, all those trials which Paul lists are the same kind of problems which the psalmist was facing. Paul is saying that Christians *will* face trouble and hardship and persecution. Even in a currently rich and relatively safe country, we might someday have to face famine, nakedness, danger, and swords. But are they an indication that we've been separated from God's love? Do they mean we've failed? Are we destined to lose? "No! In *all* these things we are *more* than conquerors through Him who loved us."

Some trials can last a long time and be tough indeed. But we can rest assured on at least three points. First, nothing will separate us from God. Second, we'll be tested and molded and stretched, but we won't be harmed. And third, the trials will be just exactly what *we need*—no more (Hallelujah!) and no less (Oh no! OK . . . hallelujah!).

How often, when we're pleading with God to stop a trial, are we really, at a deeper level, asking God to let us not grow up?

We also need to remember that many of the crushing trials have a satanic feel about them. Real, true spiritual warfare against invisible demonic hordes is a certain fact of human life. A thought that's helped me through unbelievable pressure is this: The meaning and results of this trial go far beyond me, to people I don't even know, to generations yet unborn, to unseen powers that stagger my imagination. It was so with Job. It is so with me.

How is it possible to keep our confidence in God's love when we're feeling crushed by pain? The only way is by crying out to God. That's what trials do. That's what they're *designed* to do. They bring us to the feet of Christ.

Psalm 44 ends with a prayer for help. "Awake, O LORD! Why do you sleep? Rouse yourself! Do not reject us forever. . . . Rise up and help us; redeem us because of your unfailing love." This is no weak and dainty prayer with an overly careful approach to God. This is the real cry of a heart in desperate pain, praying passionate urgent words to a real God who will hear and answer. And if we pay close attention, we may even see—perhaps months or years from now—why we needed such a long, hot time in the furnace.

Our Father knows that it's hard to be "fired." He's ready and willing to hear our concerns and complaints. He knows them anyway, so we might as well share them with Him openly. But He won't let us be tempted or challenged beyond what we can handle.

And He won't stop working on us until we're finished.

Pain Now or Pain Later

One of the stunning realities about this whole business of discipline is that the pain that comes with it is only one form of pain. In a very real sense, it's the *easiest* form.

How can that be so? Because if we won't grow, if we won't listen, if we won't be refined in the fire, the fire will get hotter. The pain will become more painful. This is so for at least three reasons.

First, the immaturity, the "babyness," the rough edges, the barnacles, will all still be with us. They can bring so much pain and misery into our lives. They are bad, unbeneficial, unconstructive habits with agonizing consequences. The Israelites fled from Egypt as unrefined slaves. They came to the border of the Promised Land—and were still unrefined slaves.

Second, God will have to "step up" the discipline. If level one won't work, then He'll go to level two. Then level three. The fire—made hotter by our own stubborn refusal to be molded—can become scorching hot until we melt. The Israelites resisted God's discipline and received more and more. They refused to see how much refining they needed in order to be ready to cross the Jordan and take the land.

Finally, if we resist long enough, we can turn the discipline into punishment. If we won't do the good that we ought to do (the Bible is *not* just talking about avoiding sin but about building something better), then at some point our resistance can turn into sin. Ultimately, anything we do that's not born of a deepening faith becomes sin and brings in a punishing fire. The Israelites, choosing to flunk God's desert school, were unprepared when faced with the faith test of their lives, the crossing of the Jordan. Unlike their crossing of the Red Sea—where, backed into a corner by Pharaoh, they had no choice—here they could decide. They chose to die a faithless death in the desert.

The choice is ours: We can choose to accept and be formed by the pain of discipline now, or we can resist and face greater and greater pain down the road.

A Condition of Deliverance

If we want to be secure throughout our troubles and delivered from them, we've been given a condition by God that's both clear and just.

That condition is this: "Blessed is he who has regard for the weak; the LORD delivers him in times of trouble." [17] What does this mean?

We should never look down on anyone undergoing a trial. We should "have regard" for them. This means we understand, we get in their shoes, we bleed with them. And we don't look down on their "dinky" trials. Perhaps this trial that seems so insignificant to us is enough to push them to the breaking point. We choose to be "merciful to those who doubt."[18]

But "having regard" means more than not looking down on others and their trials. It means we choose to encourage them, to show them how discipline is molding us "so that the lame may not be disabled, but rather healed."[19]

If we can do it, so can they—with a little regard.

The Pain Will Be Worth It

If the pain we're facing seems as big as a mountain, think how great the glory that accompanies it will be! Since the glory is always far greater than the trial, what's greater than a mountain? What level of glory is *far* greater than a mountain of pain?

That's why we should consider it pure joy when we face light and *momentary* trials. It's because our suffering is nothing compared to the *eternal* glory that it's achieving for us.

The pain *will* be worth it if we keep going. The trial *will* end at just the right time. "The God of peace will *soon* crush Satan under your feet."[20] There really is glory—*glory*—ahead.

One Christian leader has said that the beginning point of all growth is unflinching honesty.[21] When we do begin to face the truth and let God's fire purify our hearts, we become stronger people who can face the challenges of life. Whether those challenges are remembering an abusive childhood, or losing a job, or being insulted and wounded, we can face them.

We will also find that a fire is kindled within us that burns with zeal and passion for God. And when that fire burns within us, the people we meet will know one thing for sure.

They'll know they've just encountered someone who really knows the God of fire.

Part Three

The Consuming Fire of Punishment
∞

T E N

The punishment that brought us peace was upon him . . .
by oppression and judgment he was taken away.
Isaiah 53:5, 8

Jesus and Punishment

I fear God, yet am not afraid of Him.

Sir Thomas Browne

———

*H*is head was swimming.

He felt His head moving uncontrollably, rolling forward and then snapping back. The pain was unbelievable. He couldn't isolate where the agony came from—it was a pain in His whole being, ripping at every part of His body.

How long have I been here? He tried to remember, but the pain was too unrelenting and dominating. Minutes, hours—it seemed like days, like years, like forever. *When will it end?* He wanted to scream but somehow held it in.

The sounds below Him were so loud and confusing. He could hear wailing and sobbing, laughing and taunting. *What are they saying?* He tried to focus, but a sharp pain shot through His shoulders and He found Himself gasping for breath. *What are they saying?*

". . . others," He heard one man saying, "but He can't save himself!" The irony of the thought pierced Him. *I can save Myself. I can. Don't you know that I can? But if I do, what will happen to you?* ". . . save Himself if He is the Christ of

God, the Chosen One. . . . Let God rescue Him now if He wants Him." *I am the Christ. That's why I can't come down. That's why My Father won't rescue Me.*

He struggled to open His eyes. Right below Him was a slow-moving stream of people with faces shriveled into hateful sneers. Most of the sarcasm was coming from them. He lifted His eyes. There, off to His left and in the distance, were the women, so many women. He could see Zebedee's wife and Salome. He saw Mary, the mother of James the younger, lying on the ground. Then His eyes caught a penetrating stare. It was Mary of Magdala.

Even from a distance He could see the love pouring from her face. The grief in her eyes was crushing, but it was mingled with so much love. *Her face is a portrait of heaven.* Suddenly, He realized He was naked. The shame pierced Him more deeply than the torture of the cross. When He looked up again, He saw her—her body shaking—moving toward the cross. *Oh, Father,* His spirit silently screamed. *Does she have to see this?*

He looked again at her face. He saw that her eyes were locked onto His. And then He felt it, understood it, more deeply. *This is what true love looks like. She's with Me in My pain and humiliation. She understands.* He tried to smile but His face was too disfigured from the beatings. He cried as He realized that He had no smile left. She saw the attempt, and her eyes sparkled through the flow of her own tears.

He looked next to her and saw His mother and her sister. Mary the wife of Clopas was kneeling, looking up at Him. He saw John standing just behind them. He looked back at His mother and tried to find the words. "Dear woman," He rasped, "here is your son." She looked surprised and turned to face John. "Here is your mother," He said hoarsely to John. He tried to say more but swooned with the pain.

". . . You the Christ?" He heard shouted from His side. He tried to look but couldn't. *Who is that?* "Save Yourself and us!" He heard the voice taunt. He realized that it was the man on the cross next to Him. *I'm trying. I'm trying to save you. Can't you see that's what I'm trying to do? Don't you understand? Doesn't anybody understand?*

"Don't you fear God . . . ?" He heard the man on His other side yelling in a tortured voice at the first man. He tried to listen to what he was saying, but it was so hard. He pushed down with His feet and tried to tilt His head. ". . . getting what our deeds deserve. But this man has done nothing wrong."

He opened one eye. This second man had been insulting Him through the whole ordeal. There he was now, his body wrecked, his face twisted, the aura of death all around him. But his eyes, his eyes! He understands! "Jesus," the man rasped, then began coughing. "Remember me . . . when You come . . . into Your Kingdom."

Gripping pain ripped through Jesus' chest. He shuddered and tried to push Himself up again. He opened His eyes and looked at the wretched man. "I tell you the truth," He said, His voice cracking. "Today . . . you will be with Me in paradise." He watched as the man nodded and then, somehow, smiled.

I can make it. This is why I'm here. I'm doing this for them. I can make it! He looked again at the women in the distance. He could see and feel their care. *I can make it.* He looked at those beneath Him and tried to tell each one something with His eyes.

Then He focused again on the face of Mary of Magdala. She had never moved, never taken her eyes off His. He realized that she was sharing in His pain, even as her love for Him shone from her face. *Is this the same woman who screamed at Me with the voices of seven demons?* She had been so lost, so hopeless. She had known nothing of love. But she had learned, so eagerly that it had astonished Him. She had become a woman of power and purity.

Tears were streaming down her face, but her eyes were stunningly clear. He could see her forming words, silently forming words. *What's she saying? I have to know what she's saying!* He squinted His eyes and tried to focus. *I need these words, Father; I need to see these words!* Then He saw the expression and felt the words: "I love You, Master," she was saying over and over. Feeling all the love, seeing all the love, the thought came to Him again: *I can make it.*

And then everything went black.

Oh, no! Not that, please not that! He felt his spirit rebel. *Anything but that!* He looked around desperately, but it was no use. He could see nothing. *I knew the sun would stop shining, but not now! I need to see these people! I need to see the love! This is too much, too much. Oh, Father, this is too much! Can't I see those who love Me? I can make it if I can just see them. I know You have to beat Me, Father, but this too?*

He felt the blows inside His being. He could feel all of the sicknesses and diseases creeping, pouring through His body. He felt a raging fever, a throbbing pain in His ears, a ripping in His back, an irresistible urge to vomit. The physical pain of the cross faded as He felt Himself becoming a crumpled lump of torment. He panicked as He realized that He could no longer pray. Incomprehensibly, He began turning dark and ugly inside. He trembled as the blows increased immeasurably.

This is hell, He thought, as His unformed screams reverberated through the heavens.

A certainty about Scripture and life is that God is just and will hand out punishment. But it's just as certain that He also knows how to take it.

Punishment is justice. It's an unpleasant consequence of disobeying unbreakable laws. It's severe because violations against a holy God are heinous and indefensible. And it's a fire which our Father uses to wake us up to the deadliness of our ways.

Billions of people. Thousands of years. The number of sins is unfathomable. The Bible speaks of sin getting worse and worse, of evil men going from bad to worse, of sins getting heaped up to the limit. Humanity keeps running up the tab, adding to the bill, inviting more punishment. God keeps having to "hold the unrighteous for the day of judgment."[1] Sooner or later, there has to be a payday.

Payday. The good news of Scripture is not that sin—any sin, all sin—will be left forever unpunished. All sin *will* be punished. The only question is this: Will we be punished for all of our own sin, or will someone volunteer to be punished for us? But who would be so reckless as to volunteer for such a ghastly thing?

Jesus.

Whenever a deadline is approaching for something I don't like to do, I feel the pressure and tension mount. That task begins to dominate my thoughts, my feelings, my entire present. I know I have to do it, but everything inside of me wants to say no.

Imagine if we were facing the ultimate deadline.

Jesus is being blasted to pieces on a cross. He's already been betrayed and deserted by His followers, by itself a dreadful trial. He's been condemned by people who just days before wanted to make Him king. He's been beaten and clubbed, spit upon and insulted. He's been crowned with thorns and nailed to a tree. He's been left hanging, dying and naked, before both His enemies and His loved ones.

The staggering thing is that the injustice, the indignity, and the beatings were the easy part.

Those three hours on the cross, from the sixth to the ninth hour, were when Jesus wore the ultimate face of death. He was cut off from everyone and everything, as the sun itself stopped shining. For an incomprehensible moment in time, God was agonizingly split in two. He could no longer see the love and care coming from His supporters. This—the isolation, the complete aloneness, the unfixable separation—is almost a perfect picture of the hell that awaits those who don't ask that Sufferer to be their Savior and Lord.

Almost a perfect picture.

For even that wasn't the hardest part. During those hours a transformation took place—one so bizarre that our minds resist the fullness of it. Jesus stopped being a man and became sin.

The Scriptures are clear. "God made him who had no sin to be sin for us."[2] Is the Bible just using dramatic words to get our attention? No. Jesus, somehow, someway, *became* sin. "The sun stopped shining"—partly as a symbol to the people of what sin had done in darkening the whole world, partly as a way of making Jesus' suffering total, and partly because what occurred on that cross for those three hours was too hideous for anyone to ever gaze upon.

Jesus *had* to become sin. There's no other way that a just God could punish one who Himself "knew no sin." Jesus had done nothing to deserve a shred of punishment. The Bible is clear that "the soul who sins is the one who will die" and that "each is to die for his own sin."[3] Just as the one thief said, Jesus hadn't done anything to deserve punishment—while the rest of us have been asking for it our whole life long.

So Jesus had to literally *become* sin—not generic sin, but *our* sin. He had to take our place, to make a transformation, so that when God the Father looked down, all He could see was our sin. It was then that the real blows began, the blows that made what Jesus had already suffered on the cross seem insignificant by comparison.

He took every whipping, felt every clubbing, endured every disease and sickness and infirmity that ever was or will be. Because of Him, we don't need to face some horrifying version of those awful three hours for eternity (which is a very long "time"). We can choose to become Christians instead. And because of Him, we don't even need to face any more punishment here, in this life. If we've become Christians, we can let His grace teach us and empower us to live a life that needs no punishment.

Jesus got everything that sin deserves. He got everything that we deserve. It was an unbelievably big bill.

The bill has been paid.

ELEVEN

Those whom I love I rebuke and discipline.
So be earnest, and repent.
Revelation 3:19

Seven Purposes of Punishment

Punishment is a sort of medicine.

Aristotle

Cindy's motto was "Live for the moment." She enjoyed being spontaneous and loathed making plans or keeping commitments. She said whatever was on her mind, even if it was rude or damaged others. She would back off any relationship that began to make demands on her. She would set times to meet with people and be an hour late (or not show up at all) and would be angry if challenged about it. "She has no purpose to her life," people would say.

But she did. Her purpose was complex and multifaceted: to feel in control of her life; to meet her own needs first and always; and to avoid facing the misery that past relationships had caused her. Everyone around her lived with the consequences of Cindy's self-centeredness.

Sometimes our lives and the lives of those around us seem sloppy and disconnected. But even though we may not want to admit it, each word and detail has a purpose, is caused or driven by something, has some end in mind.

The purpose may be to meet some perceived need, satisfy some selfish desire, or numb some burning pain which

is warning us of a soul disease. It may be to defend ourselves when we're wrong or to destroy someone of whom
we're jealous. It can include goals like improving our own
position by tearing others down; controlling others
through manipulation; and trying to get the love we need
by taking and using rather than by giving and receiving.

All good purposes, no matter how small, will be
blessed. All bad purposes, no matter how small, will be
condemned. God at first brings punishment to free us from
our bad purposes.

Punishment Can Be an Ally—Up to a Point

The pain of discipline is always an ally. The pain of punishment can also be an ally—if we listen to it, especially in its earlier stages.

What does this mean to us? It means that punishment
is intended to turn us back to God, to life, to goodness, to
blessing. It certainly has other purposes, such as displaying
God's justice and warning other sinners. But God's goal is
restoration. Often, because we're stubborn, the only hope
of restoration is through loving punishment.

William Ernest Hocking said, "Only the man who has
enough good in him to feel the justice of the penalty can be
punished; the others can only be hurt." Punishment is always
effective justice. It's effective medicine only when we're willing to listen.

If the offense is severe, He "will not let [us] go entirely
unpunished," [1] for justice's sake and because of His law of
reaping and sowing. He can continue to give grace and
goodness, but we can resist and *need* judgment. He's patient, but if we keep going long enough, punishment will
cease to be an ally and will mean only "terror and pitfalls,
ruin and destruction." His "Spirit will not contend with
man forever."[2]

One quite troubling Scripture is Hebrews 10:26–31:

> If we deliberately keep on sinning after we have received
> the knowledge of the truth, no sacrifice for sins is left, but
> only a fearful expectation of judgment and of raging fire

that will consume the enemies of God. Anyone who rejected the law of Moses died without mercy on the testimony of two or three witnesses. How much *more* severely do you think a man deserves to be punished who has trampled the Son of God under foot, who has treated as an unholy thing the blood of the covenant that sanctified him, and who has insulted the Spirit of grace? For we know him who said, "It is mine to avenge; I will repay," and again, "The Lord will judge his people." It is a dreadful thing to fall into the hands of the living God.

Many say that this is referring to the punishment that awaits unbelievers if they refuse to repent and commit to Christ as their Savior and Lord. But if we look at this passage closely, we see that it is speaking of someone who "has treated as an unholy thing the blood of the covenant that *sanctified* him," which can only mean a believer. This doesn't mean that we can lose our position in Christ. It *does* mean that we can be punished even if we're saved.

To confirm this point, the passage goes on to say, "The Lord will judge *his people*." This message is repeated in a "warning about punishment" in 1 Corinthians 10:1–13, where we're told to learn from the experience of those who were judged. The Hebrews passage concludes soberly: "It is a *dreadful* thing to fall into the hands of the living God." At this point, punishment is no longer an ally.

Now it's an enemy, severe and implacable.

Seven Purposes

God's punishment of our evil words and actions has a number of purposes. None of the punishments of God are willy-nilly. None of them are random, arbitrary, or poorly thought-out. Let's take a look at some of the purposes our God can have in this sobering business of punishment.

1. To Turn Us Away from Wrong Paths

As we've seen in the first part of this book, God puts the thorns of stern discipline just off the side of the narrow path. These warn us to adjust our course and return to the level way. Just a little further off the path, we run into the stronger "medicine" of punishment.

Punishment is God's way of "turning up the heat." He wants us to turn away from wrong paths, to reject our sinful course, to change from a deadly path to a living way. "Your own conduct and actions have brought this upon you. This is your punishment. How bitter it is! How it pierces to the heart!"[3] Jeremiah tells us that the goal of bitter punishment is to pierce to our hearts, to blast away the stone.

God wants to wake us up and cause us to cry out to Him and avoid yet more punishment. He says, with frustration, "In vain I punished your people; they did not respond to correction."[4] His punishment has the clear purpose of correction. Punishment is a piercing knife now, so we can avoid a devouring sword later.

God's purpose is the same whether the sin is evil through-and-through or a good thing carried outside boundaries. To lust after someone, take advantage of her, use her and abuse her, is "plain old" sin. Unfortunately, this is the norm in human hearts and relationships. "'There is no one righteous, not even one.'"[5]

Christians don't always call these things what they really are. Allen was considered a "good" husband because he provided for his family, spent some time with them, did some things around the house, and rarely exploded in anger. But was this "love"? What was in Allen's heart?

Allen's real purpose was simply to have an easy life, to have his family serve him, to keep his wife under his thumb and away from ministry, and to have a good "image" with outsiders. Allen was a taker/user who wore a sign reading, "I love my family." Too much of what passes as Christian life is really a good act, a sinful masquerade.

To really love someone, on the other hand, is good (and rare). Real love is an exquisite treasure: breathtaking and delicate, durable yet fragile. It's not determined by the outward "form" of the relationship, for many spouses and siblings hate each other, while unrelated girls aged eight and eighty can share the love of a lifetime. Real love is hard to come by.

But if that love becomes more important to us than our love for God, it becomes an idol. The friendship doesn't need to be abandoned, but our hearts must be renewed and redirected so that our relationships are in the right "order." God must always be first, with all other loves based in and growing out of our love for Him. God will suffer "no other gods" before Him and will punish us for the idolatry of relationship as surely as for the idolatry of a totem pole.

Our Lord wants us to turn away from sin—whether it's the whole rotten loaf or the yeast in an otherwise nourishing batch of dough.

2. To Cut Out and Kill the Cancer in Our Hearts

Although punishment is designed to turn us from wrong paths, God wants more than momentary repentance. He wants to extinguish the spreading disease in our hearts, the cancer cells that drive the sin, the sickness fueled by hell.

Human punishment is often imbalanced and excessive. God's punishment never is. If it "feels" too heavy, it may be because we're too "soft" on our sin or too blinded by our folly. It may be that we're being punished for a whole series of sins, but we're just looking at the last one. God operates on a different principle and sometimes lets sins get "heaped up" before He punishes.

Or it may be that God is probing more deeply into the source of the sin and is trying to kill it at its fountainhead. Sometimes the punishment seems deeper than we think it should be because the cords of the sin are holding us so tightly. The tentacles of the sin have gone deep, cancerously working their way into the core of our being. The actual sin may be much worse than its outward manifestation.

Hank constantly said demeaning things and exploded in anger. Then he'd say, "I'm sorry I was angry," and get angry again because the offended person wasn't willing to forgive him. He demanded that his wife and children say the words, "I forgive you," even when they didn't believe he was repentant. Hank resented them for "punishing" him, when he hadn't even addressed the real sin—his hateful and murderous heart that spilled over in anger.

It's easy to see the surface manifestation of a sin and never deal with the deep roots. "There are a thousand hacking at the branches of evil to one who is striking at the root," Thoreau observed. We'll never have complete victory without pulling out the roots. Even removing 98 percent of a cancer may not be enough to save our life.

If we make it through God's radical surgery and allow the cancer to be removed, we can be alive and vigorous once again. If we respond properly to the firestorm of punishment, we'll be stronger, battle-hardened, "street-smart."

And wise.

3. To Cleanse and Purge Our Hearts

"Blows and wounds cleanse away evil, and beatings purge the inmost being" (Prov. 20:30).

God punishes us to turn us away from evil. He also punishes us to kill the cancer at the center of our being. He also uses punishment to cleanse the nooks and crannies of our hearts and to purge our hearts of "hidden faults."

Until the big tumors are removed, we may not be able to see the smaller ones. To us, these small sins might seem minor compared to our "whoppers." We can even convince ourselves that they aren't sins at all—just "bad habits." But no sinful cancer is minor to God.

Ted thought he was dealing with something that was problematic but not sinful. His boss was oppressive and, at times, irrational. Ted's response was to join with others in his department in ridiculing the boss behind his back. Every comment he and others made—no matter how snide—seemed justified by the boss's tyrannical directions and actions.

This wasn't the old "pre-Christian" type of sin (the wrong life path) or a cancer at the core of Ted's being (a deeply rooted and long-lasting course). This was something new. Then God's cleansing, purging fire entered the scene in the form of even more daily contact with the boss and a more oppressive work environment.

But Ted ignored God's gracious warnings and continued on his sinful path. Now he felt a heavier hand. He began battling sickness and other physical challenges as his work situation "ate" at him. Feelings of loneliness and alienation—which can be a powerful punishment—bombarded him. Doubts and fears that he hadn't felt in years surrounded his heart and felt like "the sentence of death."

Blows and wounds and beatings. They finally woke Ted up and showed him the way. He stopped complaining about his boss and began to treat him with less fear but more respect. Even though the boss had offended Ted in countless ways, Ted found a way with God's help to ask the man for forgiveness for an angry response in a meeting. His boss responded with more respect for Ted (even though the oppression continued at a lower level), and he was genuinely sorry when Ted moved on to another company. As Ted began to act correctly, he felt life pouring back into his heart.

The "many blows/few blows" principle comes into play here. Jesus tells us that deliberate disobedience of a known command will bring us "many blows." If we know something is wrong but do it anyway, we're inviting a stricter punishment. But if our sin arises from issues or areas of our heart which we don't yet see clearly, then we'll get "few blows." We'll still get punished—sin is always sin—but like Paul we'll be "shown mercy because [we] acted in ignorance and unbelief."[6]

"Forgive my hidden faults," the psalmist prays.[7] Purging fire is often what brings us to this prayer.

4. To Teach Us the Reap/Sow Principle

God has built laws into creation and life. Only He can make exceptions to these laws. People can't fly—but Philip flew from the baptism of an Ethiopian to the city of Azotus. The solar system operates dependably—but the whole thing stopped for a day when Joshua cried out for help. Everyone must die—but Enoch and Elijah skipped their own funerals and went straight on to glory.

We shouldn't depend, however, on being "excepted" from God's laws. Fooling ourselves into believing we're exceptions is equated with mocking God. "Do not be deceived:

God *cannot* be mocked. A man reaps what he sows."[8] Every action has an equal and opposite reaction. We only get out what we put in. The piper must be paid.

"Remember this," Paul tells us, "whoever sows sparingly will also reap sparingly, and whoever sows generously will also reap generously."[9] What we reap from life is related to what we sow into life. If we plant no crops, we get no harvest. If we work an hour, we can expect no more than an hour's pay. If we're lazy, "poverty will come on [us] like a bandit, and scarcity like an armed man." If we give generously, we'll "prosper" and be "refreshed."[10]

Punishment is part of the reap/sow principle. It's designed to show us that God's built-in laws work. Sometimes the punishment is built right into the sin. If we violate someone's trust, she won't trust us anymore. If we trash someone's heart, he will come to loathe and despise us. If we start a fight, we might end up getting stitches. If we take illicit drugs, we'll destroy our minds and bodies.

Sometimes the punishment is externally imposed. Children reject their parents' boundaries and get intimately familiar with the corner. Men kill in cold blood and are then executed. Those claiming to be Christian brothers live like the devil and are excluded from the church.

But while people may do a miserable job of enacting God's required punishments, God does an excellent job. He interweaves built-in punishment and externally-imposed punishment. A criminal is released from prison prematurely and gets murdered by another criminal. A woman with a surly spirit abuses her friend and then gets abused at work by her boss.

Let's not be fooled. Sin never gets "lost." We never reap more or less—or differently—than we sow.

5. To Let Justice Reign in the Universe

The reap/sow principle relates to another key principle that God has instituted: Justice will reign.

Someone once said that the only thing man learns from history is that man never learns anything from history. In successive power grabs, Charles XII of Sweden invaded Russia and failed, Napoleon invaded Russia and failed, and Hitler invaded Russia and failed. The British trusted Hitler and plunged into World War II. The West trusted Stalin and became embroiled in the Cold War. Germany bombed London and ended up shattered by British bombs. Japan bombed Pearl Harbor and ended up devastated by The Bomb.

Governments are notorious for believing that they can escape from truth, reality, and judgment. Governments think this way because as individual *people* we believe that we can escape from truth, reality, and judgment. But governments can't and neither can we. Somewhere, somehow, all sins will be punished, all wrongs will be righted, and all the unrepentant wicked will get their due. That "somewhere" includes the next life, to be sure.

And it also includes here.

"If the righteous receive their due *on earth*, how much *more* the ungodly and the sinner."[11] When it looks like sin is having its day and the wicked are flourishing, we have to realize that it only *looks* that way. "Surely you place [the wicked] on slippery ground; you cast them down to ruin. How suddenly are they destroyed, completely swept away by terrors!" "A little while, and the wicked will be no more."[12]

Punishment is God's justice working its way into life. God's basic rule is what the Bible calls *lex talionis*, the law of an eye for an eye. If someone kills someone else, our laws shouldn't just prick his finger. As individuals working for another kingdom, we may need to turn the other cheek, give away our cloak, or walk a second mile. But our forbearance doesn't mean that *lex talionis* is repealed; it doesn't mean that the striker of cheeks, taker of tunics, and forcer of walks won't be punished for his or her actions. It only means that we're leaving justice to others or Another; that we've chosen to "commit [ourselves] to [our] faithful Creator and continue to do good."[13]

A dramatic example of justice is the story of Achan in Joshua 7. After the Israelites conquered Jericho, he took things that belonged to the Lord and buried them in his tent. He was then caught, judged, and executed, along with the family that supported him in his theft. This story is bothersome in an age of cheap grace, easy-believism, and forgive-and-forget theology, because Achan is given no opportunity to "get off the hook" or to make restitution. His story would end differently if it were written by many Christians today.

But the stunning justice can't be explained away on the basis of dispensational teaching or "cultural differences" or a "God used to be tougher" mentality, for the story is repeated in Acts 5 in an incident involving a married couple, Ananias and Sapphira.

Ananias, like Achan, took things that belonged to the Lord. His method was a little more sophisticated: He claimed to give the full price of a "devoted" piece of property to the Lord, but like Achan buried some of the loot elsewhere. He, too, was given no opportunity to get off the hook or make restitution. God simply struck him dead. His wife followed him in his lie and, like Achan's family, joined him in death.

The point of these two stories? A very sobering one indeed: Don't rob God. "Will a man rob God? Yet you rob me . . . in tithes and offerings."[14] Judas took from God's purse and ended up like Achan and Ananias. Will God still eat out *our* substance and drain *our* lives away if we rob Him, if we take the "devoted" things?

"Jesus is the same yesterday and . . . ."

6. To Teach People Righteousness

God knows that we're "slow to learn," so He gives us lessons to help us. One of those lessons is punishment.

"When your judgments come upon the earth, the people of the world learn righteousness."[15] Without the intervention of divine punishment, we could go on merrily assuming that we're doing quite well, thank you, and have no need to evaluate our ways. But His judgments stop us in our tracks; they take the fight out of us. They give us the uncomfortable but necessary opportunity to learn His ways and absorb them into our ways.

Isaiah goes on in the next verse to tell us that "though grace is shown to the wicked, they do not learn righteousness." Grace is a wonderful gift. It's God's offering and granting of good things, even to the wicked who deserve no such consideration. But although grace is necessary, it isn't enough to teach wicked people righteousness. More is needed. That "more" is God's judgments on the earth.

In fact, even if judgment doesn't teach this wicked person, it may teach a second sinful person who watches the first being punished. "Flog a mocker, and the simple will learn prudence."[16] We can look at someone being punished and choose to say no to the same sin in our own lives, to gain a very practical prudence, to learn righteousness.

King Hezekiah, in his psalm of praise after recovering from a terminal illness, spoke with deep personal awareness about the teaching aspect of punishment. "I will walk humbly all my years because of this anguish of my soul. Lord, by such things men live; and my spirit finds life in them too. . . . you have put all my sins behind your back."[17] God's punishment is the way to life—for those who listen.

7. To Protect the Innocent

The Book of Esther tells the story of an official, Haman, who hates one Jew, Mordecai, and decides to "destroy all Mordecai's people, the Jews, throughout the whole kingdom." Haman draws up plans for the slaughter and erects a gigantic gallows on which to hang Mordecai. Through a remarkable series of events, Haman's plot is foiled. He is hung on the gallows and the Jews are saved. God's punishment on the wicked brings protection and life to the innocent.

"The words of the wicked lie in wait for blood." "When the wicked rise to power, men go into hiding." "Like a roaring lion or a charging bear is a wicked man ruling over a helpless people." "When the wicked rule, the people groan."[18] Wicked people seldom keep their evil to themselves; the nature of evil is to involve, pervert, and destroy others. If left unchecked, bad company corrupts much innocent character.

But, gloriously, "the righteous man is rescued from trouble, and it comes on the wicked instead." "When the wicked perish, there are shouts of joy." "Be *sure* of this: The wicked will not go unpunished, but those who are righteous will go free." "He who leads the upright along an evil path will fall into his own trap." "When the wicked perish, the righteous thrive."[19] God's punishment of the wicked positively affects the welfare of the innocent.

Praise God that He doesn't leave us at the mercy of the wicked or wickedness! The wicked may have their day and they may succeed in some of their schemes, but their punishment is sure. Let's not grieve over the death of the wicked or the punishment and curtailing of their fiendish ways. One mocker is punished, and a hundred innocents may be spared.

Jesus said, "Things that cause people to sin are bound to come, but woe to that person through whom they come." God will judge and punish everyone who causes "one of these little ones to sin."[20] He does this to protect other innocents from the same or perhaps even greater harm.

There's no question that innocent people suffer at the hands of the wicked. God's use of punishment doesn't mean that malicious people will never carry out their plans. It doesn't mean that innocent people (those not participating in the evil by choice) will never suffer. It does mean that God prevents much more evil than we actually see—and brings all the evil we do see to judgment.

―――――

Punishment is a multifaceted tool. God doesn't use it indiscriminately or unjustly but always to further His purposes in the world.

Punishment can be mild ("few blows") or severe ("many blows"). Answering its call at the earliest moment can stop the blows and keep them from progressing to fearsome levels. Ignoring its lessons is the height of disastrous foolishness.

God has some good news: We don't have to be punished at all. If we're truly Christians, we can discern the end from the beginning. We can avoid the punishment by avoiding its cause.

This, surely, is wisdom.

∽

TWELVE

Consider carefully how you listen.
Luke 8:18

Seven Wrong Responses to Punishment

God pardons those who do through frailty sin,
but never those that persevere therein.

Robert Herrick

While working on his house, Randy fell and severely injured his back. He was incapacitated for months and missed much work. Cards of encouragement came in large numbers, and many told him they were praying for a speedy recovery.

What most people didn't see—what most people never see—was the reality behind the obvious "Christian-gets-hurt-and-needs-sympathy" surface. Prior to the injury, Randy had become hardened and embittered. He had yielded more and more frequently to lust and had even involved his children in it. His relationship with his family was nonexistent, except for the part that was horrible.

Now Randy was given the opportunity, through this physical punishment, to regroup and return to the Lord. But he didn't do it. His heart didn't soften. His poor treatment of his family continued, even worsened. He used his injury as an excuse to demand favors and attention from others. His response was all wrong. The results were all bad.

As with discipline, there's only one right way to respond to punishment, but a multitude of ways to respond wrongly. Let's look together in detail at seven of them. Three of them are "passive" responses: denying, hiding, and losing heart. Three of them are "active" responses: ignoring, justifying, and comparing. But whether passive or active, the results of continuing these responses are the same. Both paths end up at number seven, a terminal response.

1. Denying

Denial that we're even being punished is one of the most common and the deadliest of responses. This was Randy's response after his severe back injury.

The sinful nature doesn't want to "face the music" and admit that bad choices can and will be punished. It denies the reality of current or impending punishment. It might even deny that there is a God, or at least One who punishes.

Jesus told the story of classic "denying," the parable of a rich fool (what a contradiction in terms!). This man was rich in stored-up material things but "not rich toward God." He was a greedy, selfish man who always put himself first. The very day of his death—his last day on earth—he was oblivious to the doom hanging over his head and was making plans for even greater greed and hoarding.

It's too easy to be like the rich fool. We're wrong but don't want to admit it or even think about it. Things may be going fairly well in our lives, and so we think we have further "evidence" that there's no punishment at hand. All that's necessary to complete the picture is to fill our thoughts and days with plans and activities to distract us from seeing God's upraised hand.

Vance had heard the same negative "story" about a long-time friend from several different sources. Instead of talking to his friend or anyone who might give insight on what really happened, Vance spent more and more time listening to those who had invented or believed the gossip. He then began not only passing along the untruths, but also "warning" people not to trust his now-former friend.

When confronted by his own pastor and his friend, he denied many things, said he "couldn't remember" to whom he'd repeated the gossip, and only admitted to a "partial mistake." He agreed to go to those with whom he had shared and withdraw his slander, but he never did. Forgetting that slander and causing division are heinous sins, Vance refused to admit the truth. He chose not to see the punishment hemming him in: loss of respect from almost everyone around him, seeds of slander that were ready to sprout and cost him his job, and a deep and costly division with his wife over his actions.

Religious leaders can actually assist people in their "denying." "They dress the wound of my people as though it were not serious. 'Peace, peace' they say, when there is no peace. Are they ashamed of their loathsome conduct? No, they have no shame at all."[1] People already denying punishment will flock to such leaders, who tell their followers—out of desire for gain of some kind—that they are really doing quite well. This is appealing because many yearn to be confirmed in their delusion.

But ultimately, it doesn't matter how well we think we're doing, or how well anyone else thinks we're doing. It only matters how we are really doing.

2. Hiding

Isaiah gives us a startling insight into our ability to "protect" ourselves from punishment, to substitute our words for God's word: "You boast, 'We have entered into a covenant with death . . . when an overwhelming scourge sweeps by, it cannot touch us, for we have made a lie our refuge and falsehood our hiding place'" (Isa. 28:15).

Isaiah gave this prophecy after the Israelites had made a treaty with the Egyptians to get their protection from the Assyrians. Instead of hiding in the Rock, they were hiding in the "lie." What was the "lie"? It was made up of several parts. First, they believed that they didn't really deserve to be punished. Second, they thought that the "danger" could be skirted by human plans and fortresses. And third, they concluded that it would work: Lies and falsehood would really protect them. Believing this is as ridiculous as thinking that hiding under our blankets will protect us from a burglar.

We can do the same thing as the Israelites. We can make plans to keep us from facing the reality that the Assyrians—God's judgments—are about to overwhelm us. We can develop friendships that won't challenge our weaknesses, but will rather confirm us in our rightness. We can involve ourselves in activities and organizations so we'll be doing our part. We can buy insurance and make investments so that we'll be secure. But if punishment from God is looming, these defenses are nothing. A manmade fortress is no fortress at all. "Hail will sweep away your refuge, the lie, and water will overflow your hiding place. Your covenant with death will be annulled; . . . When the overwhelming scourge sweeps by, you will be beaten down by it" (Isa. 28:17–18).

We can try to hide, but the punishments will still come. And "as often as it comes, it will carry you away; morning after morning, by day and by night, it will sweep through" (Isa. 28:19). Once the Assyrians begin coming, they'll batter us relentlessly until we're reduced to nothing.

And "the understanding of this message will bring sheer terror."

3. Losing Heart

There's no refuge from God's punishment except God Himself. If we deny His punishment and hide from it, we won't stop the punishment from coming. In fact, we'll actually build up an "overwhelming scourge" which will eventually pound us into the ground.

It gets harder and harder to make denial "stick." The hiding becomes fruitless as the punishments wear us down. We want to cry out, to scream, but . . . to whom? For God to help us, we'd have to admit that we've been offending Him. For God to help us, we'd have to admit that He's the One who is wounding us. For God to help us, we'd have to admit that it's *our* decision whether He uses His hand to strike us or comfort us.

We're told not to "lose heart when he rebukes you."[2] How do we "lose heart"? We lose it by the process of denial

("God wouldn't punish Christians; God wouldn't punish me") and hiding ("I've structured my heart and life to avoid 'problems'"). If we do these things long enough—while the Assyrians are massing forces right outside our gate—we'll have no choice but to lose heart.

Losing heart is the cause of so much of what is normally called "depression." We can be depressed for very understandable reasons—the death of a loved one, the relocation of a friend, the loss of a job. But sin is so rampant, and our hearts so resistant to truth, that the depression many of us feel at times is the depression of losing heart, of having our defense against truth come crashing down around our ears.

This is what Jacob felt as he prepared to meet his brother Esau many years after their bitter parting. Jacob had lived in denial about his past behavior toward his brother, and circumstances had seemed to support his basic "goodness." He had hidden from his brother with Laban and had appeared to be safe. During this time he had gotten two wives, many children, and great wealth.

But Jacob's world came apart. Laban's "attitude toward him" changed. He ended up fleeing with his wives and children. He survived the encounter with Laban only to look ahead to a "reunion" with Esau, who was coming to meet him with four hundred men. Jacob was "in great fear and distress": "I am afraid he will come and attack me, and also the mothers with their children. . . . I will pacify him with these gifts."[3] Jacob had lost heart because of his own wrong attitudes. His past had finally caught up with him.

Even at this advanced stage of rebellion, there's still hope if we'll cry out to God in Spirit and in truth. Jacob did, as his moment of great depression led directly to the turning point of his wrestling match with God. There he was, scared and alone, fear pounding in his ears and disturbing his sleep. It was just he and God. They grappled in the night—we can do this too—and Jacob, in his moment of truth, decided to hang on to God for dear life. They *wrestled*—a dirty, sweaty, hand-to-hand combat. Jacob wouldn't let go until he and God were "squared."

Our depression can work to our advantage and cause us to seek a true refuge. If we've been off the path a long time, we can—we should—still cry out to God. It won't be a gentle encounter, but we can wrestle through a long night with God and come out both battle-hardened (Jacob always limped after that encounter) and blessed again by God.

If we don't, we can eventually come to number seven on our list—and pass the point of no return.

4. Ignoring

This response and the two that follow it are on the "active" side of the ledger. In these responses we're bolder.

The first of these is simply to ignore the punishment and keep going in the wrong direction. This is the bullheaded approach, the willfully ignorant path, the sin of the "high hand." This response says, "I don't care what God or anyone else says; I don't really even want to know. I'm going to do it anyway."

Buckner followed this path repeatedly. He would see a scriptural truth, appear to try to follow it for a while, have it clash with his personal goals and evil desires, and then finally give up the truth and do what he wanted. He gave up on stewardship, as he began buying everything he wanted. He gave up on purity, as he tried to lure women into sexual conversation so they could "advise" him. He gave up on forgiveness, as he refused to acknowledge his sins against others. And he gave up on gentleness, as he blasted everyone he disagreed with—which was everyone he knew.

In one case, he actually told me, "I know what the Bible says, and I agree that's the ideal way if you 'started out' on the right foot. But I didn't, and I can't believe that God would want to deny me this desire."

He was heading for the edge of the cliff, and he knew it. What he wanted was so important to him, though, that he was willing to run up to the edge and hang on to the belief that there might be pillows down below.

"The prudent see danger and take refuge . . . ." When I saw my dad start to take off his belt, I knew he wasn't getting ready to change pants. I saw the danger and changed course (usually). ". . . But the simple keep going and suffer for it."[4] To keep going in the face of God's punishment is the height of simple-mindedness.

And a rendezvous with torment.

5. Justifying

So often we try to justify our behavior by minimizing the significance of our sin. Rather than calling it "sin," we call it a "mistake" or a "white lie." We think that God knows that we're dust, so He doesn't expect much of us. Surely what we've done isn't serious enough to cause God to punish us!

We want God to be a softer God than He actually is. We like to pretend that He isn't the awesome, mighty Creator and Sustainer of the universe who gives us every breath we take and who hates all evil. Instead, we imagine Him as a kindly Grandfather, whose only concern is our immediate gratification, or a worn-out old man who wrings His hands and laments about "the kids these days."

But the real God of the Bible has both an infinite hatred of evil and an unlimited power to destroy it wherever it exists. Although He's slow to anger and forgives wickedness and sin, He won't leave the guilty unpunished; He will follow through on the "punishment" verses.

Part of the reason why God is so intolerant of any sin at all is because He knows that sins never stay small. Almost imperceptibly, thoughts and desires become actions, actions become patterns, patterns become a diseased way of life. One of wisdom's grandest lessons is that there is no small sin. The most horrible of wrongdoings can, like a giant oak tree from an insignificant acorn, sprout from the tiniest of sins. Greed begins with the child who won't share in the nursery, not with junk-bond traders on Wall Street.

We can also "excuse" ourselves because God's standards are so "unrealistically" high. No mortal could reach them, and so we shouldn't have to try. Heaven knows how hard it is to obey! In fact, heaven *does* know, but God still has a different idea: "Be holy because *I* am holy . . . be holy in all you do."[5] Some would call this teaching "legalism," a scary word that can make us run away.

But it isn't legalism; it's the life God called us to, "that the righteous requirements of the law might be *fully* met in us." "His divine power has given us *everything we need* for life and godliness."[6] Ultimately, there's no excuse for not being holy. And we don't have to do things that will cause us to be punished.

The story of Saul in 1 Samuel 15 shows the pattern of self-justification clearly. Saul had been sent on a mission to totally destroy God's enemies. He had won the battle but hadn't followed instructions; he had destroyed only the less valuable things but saved the "juicy" things. He had become so focused on himself that he had set up "a monument in his own honor," a stench to God but somehow befitting a man who "did it his way." Samuel went to Saul to tell him that God's punishment was coming.

Saul, in an outstanding example of self-defense and excuse-making, refused to accept the reality. He started right out on the offensive: "The LORD bless you! I have carried out the LORD's instructions." When confronted with his disobedience, he explained that the "soldiers" saved the best to sacrifice to God. When challenged again, he insisted that he really had obeyed the Lord completely and that it was the "soldiers" who had kept some things alive. Only when told that he was "out" as king did he admit his sin—and then he still blamed it on his fear of "the people."

Like Saul, we can be in the midst of disobeying the Lord but claim that we're carrying out His will for our lives. We can defend our positions as "righteous." We can explain how we're doing it for God.

Even if we "admit" we've done something wrong, we can *still* keep making excuses—it was our upbringing, it was our teachers, it was our circumstances. We were just victims. "Victimization" can be the answer for everything. It's true that we've all been "victimized" to some degree, but in God's eyes, victimization explains but never excuses. Being brutalized by our parents may help explain why we do it to our own children, but will never relieve us from the consequences of having repeated the sin.

None of these excuses helped Saul. None of them will help us either.

How many sins does it take to justify God's sending a non-Christian to hell? Only one. And how many sins does it take to justify God's punishing a Christian on earth?

That's right. Only one.

6. Comparing

After we've justified, excused, and rationalized our own motives and behavior, the next step in this path of an active wrong response is to compare ourselves to everyone around us. "If you think *I* deserve punishment, you should see my neighbor! I'm a *lot* better than he is!"

We can get to the point where we no longer compare ourselves against God's standards but instead measure ourselves against the fallen people around us. If they're missing God's standards by a hundred miles and we're only missing them by ninety, we conclude that we're closer to God than they are, so we must be doing very well. In fact, we're really struggling and lost in sin and far from God—about ninety miles away.

If, on the other hand, we compare ourselves with someone who seems to be doing better than we are, we can become jealous. This can cause us to tear them down—to try to make them "smaller" so we'll feel "larger."

Jesus knew what to say to those "who were confident of their own righteousness and looked down on everybody else."[7] He knew that part of their bogus confidence came from a reduction of God's Word down to a list of rules; but He also knew that part of it came from a comparison mentality.

In response to this, He told them about a Pharisee who thanked God for the "fact" that he wasn't "low down" like the man next to him. The Pharisee didn't thank God for making the difference—he took the credit himself, listing some things he had done which made him "special." Those "accomplishments" didn't impress God.

Comparisons feed illusions, nourish negative directions, and build pride. They "work" because we can always find someone who appears to be doing worse than we are. They "work" because many people who know little about us will buy into the comparison and tell us how "great" we're doing. But being better than the devil doesn't make us an angel.

7. Becoming Stiff-necked

Whether coming from a passive or active path of wrong response, the end is the same.

The term "stiff-necked" implies that a person can come to a point where his neck is frozen. It can't move. His head can't turn. He's stuck in his current direction—immobilized, rigid, embedded firmly in folly.

How does a neck get to be stiff?

If I'm not paying attention to how I'm sitting and I slouch long enough, my neck becomes very stiff. It can become so painful to move that I avoid turning my head. I begin to look for a heating pad or some way to remove the . . . the what? The stiffness? No, my first thought is to remove the pain.

Spiritual "sitting" can have the same results. If I've sat in the "seat of mockers" for a long time, I get frozen into position. Change is very difficult and requires that I face reality and accept great pain. If I'm willing, even at this late date, to accept God's punishment for what it really is and let it wake me up, I still have hope. But it's very easy at this stage to continue blockheadedly to destruction.

"These are rebellious people. . . . They say to the seers, 'See no more visions!' and to the prophets, 'Give us no more visions of what is right! Tell us pleasant things, prophesy illusions.'"[8] Amazingly, people can "honor" God with their words even while their hearts are completely disconnected from Him. "If a liar and deceiver comes and says, 'I will prophesy for you plenty of wine and beer,' he would be just the prophet for this people."[9]

The destruction will come, and with finality. "A man who remains stiff-necked after many rebukes will suddenly be destroyed—*without remedy.*"[10] A time comes when God is no longer willing to wait for repentance. He sees the rigidity and, waiting no longer, brings judgment, justice, and pent-up punishment.

"This sin will become for you like a high wall, cracked and bulging, that collapses suddenly, in an instant."[11] Pharaoh was stiff-necked and wrecked his kingdom. King Belshazzar was stiff-necked and saw the writing on the wall the very day that he was killed. Herod was stiff-necked and got eaten by worms.

We human beings have an incredible capacity to withstand pain and to adjust to discomfort. This capacity to tolerate pain serves us well when we're standing up under the trials of life or suffering for the kingdom. But when we misuse pain tolerance—when we use it to help us withstand God's warnings and lesser punishments and instead adjust to a reckless and disastrous course—we're in danger of being burned by God's punishing fire.

We must purpose together, you and I, not to fall for one of the great lies of our day, that God won't punish His children. It's all too easy to protest, "It's not my fault!" or to assure others, "It's not your fault!"

But in our own lives, if we're honest, we must admit that many things *are* our own fault. A marriage which is punishment and not pleasure still required an "I do." Children who spit on our values were raised somewhere. Anger or lust passed down to us didn't have to be accepted and nurtured. Yes, there are reasons and explanations. But some things are simply our fault.

God wants us to see Him in His full array. He is lover, forgiver, discipliner—and punisher. It's part of who He is and part of what we need Him to be. His call to us is to embrace Him in His Fatherly roles of Discipliner and Punisher. He doesn't punish us gleefully, as some perverted human parents do; but even though He does it soberly, He makes no apologies for it.

And He calls us to respond properly to His punishment. He's a gracious God, slow to anger and abounding in love. He looks at our hearts and works with us when we're struggling. He knows how hard it can be to change and gives our intentions and desires to change great weight. But He calls us to struggle through our disobedience and really change. He calls us to respond properly to His punishment.

The consequences of *not* responding properly are just too great.

THIRTEEN

*The Lord knows how to rescue godly men from trials
and to hold the unrighteous for the day of judgment,
while continuing their punishment.*
2 Peter 2:9

Ten Consequences of Responding Wrongly to Punishment

Though the mills of God grind slowly,
yet they grind exceedingly small.

Henry Wadsworth Longfellow

God tells us that He esteems anyone who is "humble and contrite in spirit, and trembles at my word."[1] He's not looking for people who can solve all of their own problems or cleanse themselves of their own sins. Such people really don't exist—they can't do these things—and their arrogance blocks them from the one response that God wants.

We can be in a sorry state. "Our sins are higher than our heads."[2] We have "hidden faults" that we're too dense to even see. When we finally come to the point where we can say, "I'm troubled by my sin," we're *already* on the right path. Even if we don't know exactly what the scope of the problem is or what changing our direction even looks like, we can be sure that we'll get a tender response from God and all the help we need.

Please note God's response if we're even *willing* to be humble and contrite. He *esteems* us! He holds us—little bitty beings floundering around in confusion—in high regard. His response is stunning. Just to have regard for us would be more than we deserve. To have *high* regard? The thought stretches our minds to the breaking point. God's love and graciousness truly must know no limits.

God is so willing to help us with the process of humbling ourselves and becoming contrite. As we begin talking about the consequences of wrong responses to His punishment, we have to understand and remember that He's our Father, that His goal is restoration, and that He doesn't snuff out smoldering wicks. Persisting in stony-heartedness will take us through this list of consequences right up to the horrific end, but any real crying out to God or move in His direction will bring Abba's help instead.

1. Direct Losses

The first consequence of not responding properly to punishment is that we reap more of what we have sown.

A man is greedy. He hoards wealth and finally the moths and rust wipe him out. If, like Zacchaeus, he responds properly—if he repents of his idolatrous greed, makes restitution, and looks for ways to help people with his wealth—he can begin to prosper again.

But if he persists in his folly, he'll reap ever-greater losses. He's robbed. He's cheated. Investments turn sour. His children are demanding and don't appreciate anything they have. He has to spend his money to bail a profligate son out of trouble. He becomes fearful of losing the rest of his precious hoard and doesn't make the investment of a lifetime. His fretting about his money shortens his life. His estate is chewed up by taxes and losses and administrators.

He can wake up—perhaps quickly, but probably gradually. Unlike Scrooge, stingy people seldom if ever get visited by beings from the supernatural realm. The story of the rich man and Lazarus teaches that it wouldn't cause the rich man to change anyway. But something can happen: He overhears a stinging insult; he's diagnosed with a severe illness and realizes that money can't assure healing; he feels a sickening emptiness that won't go away. A process is born. If he follows through, he can toss out his false god and drive the moths away.

Or, through all of this, he can refuse to see the light. He can think his problems are just "bad luck." He can rage at banks, businesses, government, doctors, and God. He can conclude that he isn't holding on to his money tightly enough and become even greedier. He ends up not being able to enjoy the thing that has become his god.

Stony-heartedness brings its own ugly "rewards." The losses may be many and unrelenting.

And can come from our very own hand.

2. Loss of Discernment

Persistence in sin begets blindness.

"Evil men and impostors will go from bad to worse, *deceiving and being deceived.*"[3] If we start out deceiving others about our sin, we'll end up being duped by others about their sin. There's no way to see clearly with a cloudy heart.

David, a mighty king who saw indisputably into the heart of God, experienced this consequence firsthand. He yielded to lust and topped it off with murder. The result? He became the very person whom his son Amnon used as a messenger to put Tamar (David's own daughter) in the position of being raped. David couldn't see it at all. Later, when another of his sons wanted to kill Amnon for raping Tamar, David was used again as the messenger to set up the murder. He didn't see that one either.

Sin makes us fuzzy. If we persist in folly, as David did, it makes us very fuzzy indeed. Sin can be sprouting all around us and we won't pick up the scent. We won't see it in our children. We'll miss it in our friends. Like David, we may even end up being used for evil purposes.

Our discernment can fade not only in relation to others, but also in relation to ourselves. It's hard enough to see our damaging ways when we have clear eyes. If we've darkened our hearts, it becomes even more difficult. Sin begets blindness, and blindness begets more sin.

3. Fear

Sin leads to fear. "The wicked man flees though no one pursues."[4] Something deep inside a wicked man tells him that somebody or something is following him.

We know we're facing punishment—that we're on a desperately wrong path—when abiding fear lurks in our heart. God is very clear that "fear has to do with punishment," including an enslaving "fear of death"—the punishment to end all punishments.[5]

We always know, if we're honest with ourselves for even a moment, when this fear is there. We can rationalize and justify and excuse, but the fear never disappears. It comes to us in unguarded times with a gripping force that can leave us terrified and joyless. It's a gnawing feeling that our heart isn't right, that something bad is coming, and that when it comes, we'll deserve it—and we'll have no way out. That's the worst of it: the unkillable "certainty" that our God won't come when we cry out for help.

The fear can be about tangible things—like death, sickness, or loss of job—or it can be an unnamed panic, a soul-queasiness, that leaves us sweaty and feeling an aloneness that is unthinkable, intolerable, unbearable.

I remember feeling such a fear once when I was alone in a large house at night. It was in a safe, affluent neighborhood. There was no logical reason to fear. But my heart wasn't right with God, and I locked and barricaded my bedroom door. I lay there, waiting, dreading the someone—the something—that I could feel in the hallway.

No one was out there. But when we're out of sorts with God, it doesn't matter. All of us are afraid at times, but if our hearts are right with God, we can trust Him and rest without fear in His perfect love. If our hearts aren't right—if we're inviting punishment—then we do have reason to hear the horrifying voice of fear.

4. Shame and Humiliation

Experiencing losses. Losing discernment. Becoming fearful. But that's not all. Shame awaits the person who persists in folly. The folly itself deserves a certain measure of shame and humiliation. "There is nothing hidden that will not be disclosed, and nothing concealed that will not be known or brought out into the open." We're told that "his malice may be concealed by deception, but his wickedness will be exposed in the assembly."[6]

Given human tendencies to love gossip and to spear the wounded, the level of shame and humiliation can be raised several levels. The slander from others drove David a number of times in the psalms to cry out to God to avenge him from his detractors, even while he acknowledged his sin. We live in a fallen world where people are willing to pile slander on top of shame, their sin on top of ours—even when they have done no better.

God allows this to happen in order to help us—and others—see the end of our path. Humiliation awaits the person who will not be humbled. Scripture and history are full of examples of people who not only persisted in sin, pride, and arrogance, but also elevated themselves until there was nothing left but shame. People built a mighty tower and ended up in a babbling confusion. Jezebel killed God's prophets and was eaten by dogs. Nebuchadnezzar was captivated by his own glory and ended up eating grass for seven years.

Hitler proclaimed a kingdom that would last a thousand years and committed suicide in the midst of its destruction after only twelve. Marx's vision and Lenin's twisted version of it lie in ruins. The British empire, at a pinnacle of power and pride, gave in to a ragtag American guerilla army. America itself, at a pinnacle of power and pride, gave in to a ragtag Vietnamese guerilla army.

No one involved planned any of these humiliating disasters. They were instead the logical, reap/sow conclusions to really bad plans. The call to us is clear. If we're wrong, we need to ask God to help us stop. If we aren't sure, we need to ask God to help us see. If we think it's a mix, we need to ask God to help us sort.

The best time is before the shame and humiliation.

5. Separation and Wandering

The sting and exhaustion of shame can lead to the terror of separation and wandering.

Separation is *required* by the Scripture when someone who claims to be a Christian has persisted in sinful folly. We're told not to "associate" or even "eat" with such people. We're also told to "judge" and "expel" them from the church. Separation, like shame, becomes both punishment and shock treatment.

The worst separation, however, isn't from people but from God. In fact, if we're separated from God, we can't help but be separated from people. Ultimately, the only thing we have to do is give account to God. His opinion is the only opinion that matters. If we're cut off from Him, we're cut off from life itself—from peace and rest and assurance and confidence. Separation from God ends up being a separation from our very selves.

This separation can lead to a wandering life. We can wander from city to city, career to career, relationship to relationship, church to church, exciting event to exciting event, teaching to teaching. We try to fool ourselves that we're only looking for "truth" or "reality," but our very drivenness to wander can be a punishment from God.

Wandering leaves us alone, lonely, alienated, empty. We can cover our emptiness with talk of being "missionaries," of "just following the Lord," of letting the Lord "lead us to the promised land"; but the reality will gnaw at our souls.

The Jews wandered for forty years in a "trackless waste." Many Christians—and those who claim to be Christians—are also wandering in a trackless waste.

They just don't see the sand.

6. Bitterness

We recoil when we taste something that's really bitter. We don't want it to stay in our mouths or go down our throats. Somehow we know instinctively that we aren't supposed to eat such a thing.

Sinful folly, too, can become bitter and distasteful. The very thing we thought we wanted leaves us gagging and unable to swallow. The formerly sinful pleasure now sickens us like a poison. We can hate it—and ourselves—even while we're still participating in it. We can come to the point of not seeing any remaining value and resenting our own life choices.

These maladies come from a heart in profound disarray. They're the end product of a long line of bad choices.

They're a punishment, and no "treatment" or multistep plan is enough to deal with their unrelenting gnawing.

When we've lived with bitterness long enough, without hearing or responding, we can end up pessimistic and cynical. *Everything* tastes bad. We can't seem to get a "little happiness" out of anything. What's God's challenge at this desperate time?

"Consider then and realize how evil and bitter it is for you when you forsake the LORD your God."[7]

A bitter-tasting path is hard to swallow.

7. Rotting

"When I kept silent [about my sin], my bones wasted away," David confesses.[8]

Sin eats us up from the inside out. It starts with our hearts and eventually affects our bodies. "Envy rots the bones."[9] At one point in my life when I had wandered from the Lord, I remember feeling like my body was being eaten up. I was always battling this or that physical problem, some of them serious. Terrible allergies, kidney stones, haunting dizziness—all assaulted me.

Sin gets a "payday." We all like paydays, but not this kind: "The wages of sin is death."[10] The pay for our sin is death—of mind, of heart, of will, of soul, of life itself. Wicked people "groan" because their "flesh and body are spent."[11] Like a slug, they shrivel and lose their substance even as they move along.

A joyous, cheerful heart, on the other hand, works like a medicine. I've come to believe that this "medicinal effect" includes positive physical improvements. But the reverse is also true. Envy, sin, evil—they all rot the bones.

Medical science, even with all of its wondrous skills, is no defense against this disease of the soul.

8. Judgment and Loss

The first seven consequences are terrible enough. The last three move to another level of severity. "It is a dreadful thing to fall into the hands of the living God."[12]

Persistence in stony-heartedness is characteristic of this advanced stage of punishment. The bitterness and cynicism turn to mocking God—if not outwardly so other people can hear, at least inwardly. Part of the mocking is in thinking that we can do as we please and not reap what we sow. The other part is in the thoughts and attitudes we have toward the One who will not let Himself be mocked.

What kinds of thoughts and attitudes? "The fool says in his heart, 'There is no God.'" Or "he says to himself, 'God has forgotten; he covers his face and never sees . . . He won't call me to account.'" How does "the One enthroned in heaven" respond? "The Lord laughs at the wicked, for he knows their day is coming."[13]

The Scripture gives an interesting picture of the three major levels of sinful degeneration. First we "*walk* in the counsel of the wicked"—we travel with the wrong crowd and follow their harmful teachings. Then we "*stand* in the way of sinners"—we stop and plant our feet in a sinful activity. Finally, at the end, we "*sit* in the seat of mockers"—we get comfortable in our sin, we "settle in," and our hearts turn toward rejection of the One who has been trying so hard to keep us out of the mocker's seat.[14]

The result? "Now stop your mocking, *or your chains will become heavier.*"[15] At this point we've already waded through many levels of punishment without reconsideration or change. We already have "chains" binding us—the chains of our sins and the chains of the punishment that go with them. If we persist, these chains of sin and punishment will get heavier and heavier.

Such a hardened condition deserves judgment. To break out of it requires a dramatic shock. The judgment, the shock, can come in many forms: famine, disease, assault, curses. The Israelites ignored God's seventh-year Sabbath law for 490 years—a total of seventy Sabbath years left unobserved. The judgment? They went into captivity for seventy years so the land would get justice and the rest due it. They didn't get away with anything. The "bill" was being carefully added up and recorded all along.

Could the same be true for us? God commands His people to take a Sabbath rest, to cease from our labors, to "have the wisdom to show restraint,"[16] to make room in our thoughts for Him. Could we suffer a loss of days as a result of our ignoring His Sabbaths? Could He take out the missing, unobserved days at the end, shortening our life? "The length of our days is seventy years—or eighty, *if we have the strength.*"[17] A Sabbath is a renewal that allows us to have the strength. Ignoring it could lead to the same judgment as the Israelites.

We, God's people, must remember that we're not "immune" because of our position. "The Lord will judge his people." "It is time for judgment to begin with the family of God." "From everyone who has been given much," He warns us, "much will be demanded."[18]

9. Wrath

If we're so hardheaded and hardhearted that we refuse to heed God's punishment, we'll eventually face God's wrath. Wrath is "intense anger or indignation." It is a "band of destroying angels."

God's wrath is different from the punishment we've discussed so far. When God punishes us, He gives us a measure of what we justly deserve in the hope that we'll respond by turning from our sin. There's still a relationship, although strained, between us. When God's *wrath* comes, on the other hand, we learn "what it is like to have me [God] against you."[19] We're driven from the presence of God, just like Adam and Eve were from the garden of Eden.

What does this mean? Well, it doesn't mean that a true Christian can lose his standing with God. We have every reason to believe that Adam and Eve repented and made it to a heavenly reward. Samson fell under great wrath, but God still heard him at the end and allowed him a great victory in his death. We're not talking about assurance of salvation here.

We're talking about assurance of wrath.

How great is God's wrath? It's "as great as the fear that is due [him]."[20] How much fear is due Him? Total. How much wrath can He have? If He is for us, nobody can stand against us. But if He is against us, nobody can help us.

As a person moves toward wrath, God—stunningly—can begin to harden the heart that has been hardening itself, as He did with Pharaoh. We can't challenge God when He does this; He's God, and He "hardens whom he wants to harden."[21] But He's eminently fair and just. He never does this to anyone who still has a "soft spot" in his heart. If someone has taken the mocker's seat and has chosen to sit there long enough, God can simply tie him to the chair of his own choosing.

And then He flogs the mocker—for justice, but not primarily for the mocker's benefit. He flogs so that others who are watching—the "simple"—will wise up and change their ways. Perhaps someone who is walking "in the counsel of the wicked" will see God's wrath and change. "The survivors of your wrath are restrained."[22]

We can, terribly, become a storehouse for God's wrath: "Because of your stubbornness and your unrepentant heart, you are storing up wrath against yourself for the day of God's wrath."[23] "Storing up wrath" means that we might not see all of the results of our actions and all of the corresponding wrath immediately. The wrath can accumulate, like an army massing for an attack. This "delayed reaction" can contribute to our self-deception, but it won't reduce the wrath itself.

God's call is to "see to it that you do not refuse him who speaks. If they did not escape when they refused him who warned them on earth, how much less will we, if we turn away from him who warns us from heaven?"[24] Life is serious—every thought, every decision, every action, every omission. We don't live in a vacuum, free to do whatever we want and somehow avoid the reaping. If we're hardened, the wrath is piling up a storehouse of terror. Hardening of the arteries is a scary thing.

But not half as scary as hardening of the heart.

10. Consuming Fire

If we ignore God's wrath and still refuse to repent and turn from our sin, we will eventually face consuming fire. This is the time when "punishment has reached its climax."

Right before the fiery blast comes in full, God's "hand is lifted high, but they do not see it."[25] They're about to be consumed by the fire reserved for God's enemies, but their hearts have cataracts—they've become spiritually blind.

God's consuming fire is not *different* from His glory. His consuming fire is part of His glory. "To the Israelites the glory of the LORD looked like a consuming fire on top of the mountain."[26] His jealousy for His people's affection is the driving force behind His fire. "The LORD your God is a consuming fire, a jealous God."[27]

When this consuming fire comes in this life, God tells us that the sights we see will drive us mad. "The LORD will send fearful plagues on you and your descendants, harsh and prolonged disasters, and severe and lingering illnesses . . . every kind of sickness and disaster . . . until you are destroyed." He then says something that sounds "unbiblical" to our "soft" version of Christianity: "Just as it pleased the LORD to make you prosper . . . so it will *please* him to ruin and destroy you."[28]

That *can't* be in the Bible! How could God come to the point of being *pleased* to destroy His very own people? He can come to this point because we can drive Him to it. He can be pleased because justice is being done. He can rejoice because the stench of ongoing sin is removed from His nostrils. He doesn't apologize for this role: "When disaster comes to a city, has not the Lord caused it?"[29]

When this consuming fire comes to us as we stand before God's throne, it will have two different effects depending on which judgment we participate in. If we're at the great white throne judgment of those who never accepted the Messiah as their own, the consuming fire will devour us in the darkness forever. If we're at the judgment where God dispenses His rewards to His people, the consuming fire will devour all of our worthless efforts, while we go into heaven with the blessings for our remaining works (if any)—and with our lives.

In a certain sense, each of us has been "a burning stick snatched from the fire."[30] The only hope for those who have never entered into a relationship with the Messiah is to cry out to Him and have Him pull them out.

For those of us who are in a true relationship with God, our goal is to walk wisely so that we'll not walk back into the fire. We must "worship God *acceptably* with reverence and awe, for our God is a consuming fire."[31]

"See, the Name of the LORD comes from afar, with burning anger and dense clouds of smoke; his lips are full of wrath, and his tongue is a consuming fire. His breath is like a rushing torrent, rising up to the neck. He shakes the nations in the sieve of destruction; he places in the jaws of the peoples a bit that leads them astray. . . . The LORD will cause men to hear his majestic voice and will make them see his arm coming down with raging anger and consuming fire" (Isa. 30:27–28, 30).

We want to hear God's majestic voice. We want it to be full of passionate fire, protective fire, everlasting fire.

But not consuming fire.

If we look at punishment from God's perspective, we can see that He has to do it to remain true to Himself. But He also has to do it to remain true to us.

He wants us to see punishment as a clear, strong reminder that our lives aren't going very well. Is that good news? It is if we consider the alternative: wrecking our lives and our futures. From this perspective, even punishment—at least as long as we can still see at all—should be received with gratefulness. Our God loves us too much to let us live an unhindered life of folly.

God disciplines us to make us stronger and more sure. He punishes us to make us weaker—or rather, to make us see how really weak we are—and to make us far less sure of where we're heading.

FOURTEEN

*Take your evil deeds out of my sight! Stop doing wrong,
learn to do right!*
Isaiah 1:16–17

The Right Response to Punishment

It would be better to eschew sin than to flee death.

Thomas à Kempis

*T*he Bible urges us to throw off the sin that so *easily* entangles us. The picture that comes to mind is of webs and vines covering our racecourse, waiting to trip us as we run the race of faith.

Does sin easily entangle? Paul said, "When I want to do good, evil is right there with me" (Rom. 7:21). We can be trying to show love to a person, and an awful thought can come into our head about that person—some old wrong is remembered or some temptation comes into our mind. Sin is all around, and it *easily* entangles us.

Sometimes I'm having a quiet time with the Lord—studying the Bible, meditating on it, and praying—and suddenly a temptation comes into my mind. I'm incensed by it! How did that get in here? Why *now,* when I'm spending time with the Lord? But think about it from Satan's perspective. When will he most likely want to distract me and cause me to stumble? When I'm meditating on Scripture and praying. I'm going to have to fight through that temptation, that sin which is waiting to entangle me.

How do we recognize the sin that so easily entangles? This discernment comes in part from punishment. God punishes us until we admit we've left His path and choose to change our course.

How do we free ourselves from the entangling vines of sin after they've tripped us up? We can't do it. Instead, we have to cry out in repentance because only God can remove our foot from the snare. We can't fight our way out of the sin; we need to stop and repent and let God get us out of the web.

I once watched an insect caught in a spider's web. The spider, who was so little compared to me but so big compared to his prey, was relentless. The little insect was caught. There was no way for it to get out of that web without intervention by someone bigger than that spider.

I could almost imagine the little insect shrieking, "Get away from me! I'm going to fight you! You're not going to get me!" Yet the more he struggled, the more entangled he became in the sticky web. Was the spider impressed by the bug's feistiness? Did that kicking and flailing keep him away? No! The bug had no chance. He was going to be the spider's lunch unless someone more powerful than the spider came to his rescue.

As a young Christian, I was like that bug. I was taught that I had been saved by grace from the penalty of sin, and now I should go "be a good person." So I went out and tried to be a good person. It didn't work out too well. Along would come a temptation, and flop, I would fall. I'd get back up, try to be a good person, and flop. Get back up again, try to be a good person again, and flop again. I was like that little insect, shrieking, "Satan, you're not going to get me this time!" But as long as I fought him in my own strength, I couldn't defeat him.

What I needed to do was to cry out to God to pull me out of the web and "zap" that spider—Satan—for me. That was the only way I could be delivered from sin.

Before we talk about how to stop the sinning that leads to punishment, let's discuss a critical first step.

Wanting to Give Up Sin

The place where sin's doom begins is in our desires.

Desire is the driving force of all of life. Everyone is driven by desires—some glorious, some reasonable, some not helpful, some hurtful, some positively destructive. We can be driven by good and bad desires at the same time—even about the same thing. Understanding and sorting out our desires is the starting point of sin's defeat.

"Each one is tempted when, *by his own evil desire*, he is dragged away and enticed." Satan and the world around us can surely bring us temptations to feed our evil desires, but these enemies can't make us sin. Only when we ignore God, His Word, our conscience, and past evidence that sin leads to death, and say yes to the evil desires, do they "conceive" and "give birth to sin."[1]

Notice that evil desires work two ways. They "drag" us away, which shows that they do have power and can pull us along a bad path. They have "punch." But they also "entice." They tease us, allure us, and try to make us believe that our lives will be wonderful if we just "let loose." It's this double effect of evil desires—the one-two punch of dragging and enticing—that makes them such a powerful enemy, so that we can find ourselves doing the things that in our inner being we don't want to do at all.

Sin's defeat begins with recognizing these evil desires for what they really are. We must actually *want* to give up our evil desires and set our hearts and minds on things above. We must be convinced in our hearts that the evil desires *are* evil. If we're not willing to admit that or if we play around with the idea that they aren't "too bad," we'll never be willing to fight the sin that flows from them. Only seeing sin as the ugly, destructive evil that it really is will give us the driving force to ever want to quit it.

This need to see sinful desires as sinful means we have to look deeply into our own hearts. The process of thinking about the driving forces of our hearts can be greatly aided by making sure we have the quiet time to do this very important work. The key questions?

- What *are* these desires that are driving me?
- Why do I want these things?
- Why do they have such an overwhelming grip on me?
- Where are these desires taking me?
- How do I feel when I get there?

If we'll ask these questions, write down in detail what we discover, and meditate on the answers, we'll have a good start toward victory. Then we should search the Bible to see what God has to say about these specific evil desires—their nature, how they work, what their effects are, how to beat them. It's amazing what this method can do to expose our true desires and start us on a winning path.

After we've done this serious work on our own before God, it could be useful to review our thoughts with a trusted friend or counselor. They can draw out issues which we haven't explored fully, give us advice on how to handle these desires, and help us see where we might have an overactive conscience.

To be effective, this search has to be done *deeply* and *thoroughly.* To say we have a desire to be gentle is not enough if we have a more entrenched desire to control others or keep them at a safe relational distance with anger. We might be teeming with conflicting desires of varying intensities, and only the courage to get them all on the table can get us started on the road to victory.

A number of men I know probed their own hearts in the area of lust. They began to see that their desire to use women came from an emptiness within, a sense of worthlessness, a feeling that they could never really be loved and appreciated for who they were. They realized that it had been easier to use pornography, the images that are drowning our culture, and women themselves for relief of the ache in their souls, rather than becoming whole people who could really love and be loved.

They saw that the more they had yielded to this desire, the stronger lust's grip had become. They felt enslaved by the lust, like they no longer had any voice in the matter. They saw the repetition of sin and felt like a dog returning to its vomit.

The results were the same: guilt, shame, a sense of being "trash," self-hatred, and then giving in again as the desire came back to drag and entice.

We have to see sin for what it really is and for where it will really take us. We must come to hate the evil desires of our sinful nature and sin itself, without coming to hate ourselves or our inner being. We must admit to God and ourselves that living life as a slave to sin isn't really living at all. We have to *want* to stop.

Sin includes the area of good things overflowing their boundaries. Some sins are hideous from start to finish—lust, rage, greed. Other activities are good in themselves, within proper boundaries—eating and enjoying our food without yielding to gluttony; being righteously indignant without yielding to anger and slander; saving for our future without yielding to pride or materialism. We should want all of the good and none of the things that can clutter it up or ruin it. "You *can* have too much of a good thing," a friend once wisely advised me.

To mature, we must face our desires. If we're honest, willing, and asking, God will help us see them clearly. Without pretending. And without giving in.

Living as a New Creature in Christ

The next step is to learn to live as a "new creature in Christ." What does this mean?

- *Becoming a Christian*. We're not Christians because our parents were, because we go to church, because we give mental assent to a set of doctrines or rules, or because we avoid the "really bad" sins. We're Christians only if we've "done business" with the living God—if we've intimately received Christ as our Savior and Lord and surrendered control of our lives to the Holy Spirit. It doesn't matter if anyone else thinks we've done this—it only matters that we've really done it.

- *Repenting of sin*. This means we turn our face away from the old path and really set our face in a new direction. We say "Enough!" and really mean it. We may not even see all of our sin right now; but we know that whenever we see it, we'll be ready for it to go. It also means that the sin actually begins to lose its grip, rather than merely causing us to feel "bad" about it while it continues unabated.

- *Confession.* This means that we agree with God that we have sin lurking within us. And we don't just agree about what the sins are, but also about how *serious* they are—how deeply entrenched and how destructive they've been to others. If this process is real, it's a lot lengthier and more traumatic than the typical "Romans Road" tract approach.

- *Weeping the right way.* There's worldly sorrow and godly sorrow. Worldly sorrow says, "I'm sorry I got caught," or "I don't like these consequences," or "I'm tired of being punished," but isn't sorry about the stoniness of heart or the true effects of the sin. It says, "I'm sorry," but keeps doing the same thing over and over again. It uses up the 490 (seventy times seven) times and then some. It changes nothing and only leaves regret. "They do not cry out to me from their hearts but wail upon their beds," the Lord says.[2] Godly sorrow is different in kind. It weeps about the rotten desires and gripping evil that drive the action. It wails about the damage to God's name and to our relationship with Him and others. It's ready to go into action, to see dramatic change, to do what it takes to be *different* and not just "improved."

- *Making restitution.* Repentance is becoming a forgotten part of much modern teaching on forgiveness, but restitution has long been forgotten. "Give everyone what you owe him. . . . Let no debt remain outstanding."[3] If we truly want a new life, we must be willing to make amends wherever and whenever we can. If we've stolen, we must not only stop stealing and request forgiveness; we must also return what we've stolen, with the proper biblically-required multiple. If we've hurt someone, we must pay for his medical care and lost wages. If we've destroyed someone's heart with rage and malice, we must find unseen ways of serving him, resist using pressure ("I asked you to forgive me; you have to"), and accept that he may forgive us but never trust us again. If we have children, we must pay as much for their care after we've divorced and left home as we would have were we still at home, even if we have to live in abject poverty as a result. Christ paid the eternal penalty for our sin, but that in no way voids our need to make restitution.

- *Relying on the Holy Spirit.* To tell someone, "Just stop doing it," is worthless. Of course they should stop sinning, but only telling them to do so isn't enough. Willpower isn't enough. People who are told this end up feeling defeated. They *are* defeated. Some churches make up lists of "rules for right living," but the Bible is clear that such rules "lack *any* value in restraining sensual indulgence."[4] Only throwing ourselves on the Lord in faith and letting His Holy Spirit fight the battle will work. Like the bug in the web, we must fix our eyes on Someone who can shred the web that entangles us and the spider who wove it.

- *Forgetting what is behind.*[5] This *doesn't* mean that we refuse to face the depths of our sin and its effects, or offer cheap repentance, or expect cheap forgiveness, or avoid making restitution, or get upset if people remember what we've done, or lose sight of how easily we can fall. Instead, "forgetting what is behind" means that we don't let previous falls keep us down. We're like the great quarterback, Joe Montana, who was able to "go out and forget about his last bad play, and attack the next play with a fresh attitude." He was immensely successful—not because he never made mistakes, but because he never let the mistakes kill him. "A man is not finished when he is defeated," one president said. "He is finished when he quits."

- *Resisting the sinful nature, the world, and the devil.* The waves of temptation will come. When they do—at that moment, not two hours before or after—we have a decision to make: Will we give up and give in, or will we fight like heaven? Heaven has enough power to help us win a hundred times out of a hundred. At that moment, will we believe it and claim it?

We become a new creature in Christ positionally when we finally take our death-grip off our lives and turn them over to God. That's what happens when we take the first step above. But we become a new creature in Christ in our daily lives and inner character when we make all the rest of the steps a habitual part of our existence.

Hope for the Person Who Truly Stops

At least three outstanding things happen when we stop sinning.

First, God will forgive us and stop punishing us. We've allowed God to give us back our lives, to really live again. Peace, assurance, security, and confidence can fill our hearts once more and enrich our lives beyond anything we might imagine. When we stop, God stops too.

Second, our relationship with God is restored. "If I had cherished sin in my heart, the Lord would not have listened."[6] God will choose to hear us again. We can hear Him again. We've stopped being part of the problem and have become part of the solution. God can now fashion disciplines to hone us and make us useful. He can bless us and reward us for our labors for Him. We can have overflowing joy at the center of our beings.

Third, we've created the opportunity to restore what's broken in our lives—broken hearts, broken relationships, broken situations—or to build something that was never there in the first place. It's only an opportunity and not an "automatic"—for as we've seen, all actions have consequences. We still may have to face the consequences of our actions, perhaps for a long time.

A man is killed by a drunk driver. The murdered man had no savings or insurance, and his family is now in desperate need. The drunk driver needs to grieve and repent, but this won't bring the man back to life or provide for his family. The drunk driver needs to make restitution, which in this case could be enormous and ongoing. And even if that step is taken, the drunk driver may have to live with the fact that the dead man's family may never choose to forgive the brutal and incomprehensible offense.

Tina slaughtered the hearts of her children with her rage and insults. She was encouraged to change but wouldn't. Her husband was approached about the problem but chose not to intervene. Now the children hate her. She needs to grieve and repent, but this won't bring her relationship with them back to life. This assassin of hearts needs to make restitution, but what's the price for a murdered heart? It could be even more enormous and ongoing than the drunk driver's. "Though many can forgive injuries, *none ever forgave contempt,*" said Benjamin Franklin.

With Christ's help even contempt can be forgiven, but it's a mighty mountain to scale. It *must* be forgiven if the offender has genuinely repented. But even if those whose hearts have been ripped to pieces do forgive, they may never again be able to trust the person who did it. In fact, if the change in the slayer's heart hasn't been real and all the way to the core, they *shouldn't* trust her again. Damaged, closed hearts are a terrible consequence of sin, and the road to forgiveness is not through a two-minute conversation. The road between forgiveness and trust may be even longer, with chasms too wide to bridge.

We aren't talking here about a decent relationship being hopelessly wrecked by a single comment. God's power to heal and restore is vast and can work fairly quickly where the core relationship is strong. And we aren't talking about someone who has never really repented but makes grand claims of change (which are really delusions, lies, and manipulation). We're speaking here of a massive destructive act or an ongoing defective way of life. In such a case, where the damage may be incalculable, the way back to trust (as opposed to forgiveness) may be longer than a lifetime.

With that said, we need to emphasize that the *opportunity* for reconciliation is there as a result of our godly sorrow, true repentance, and willingness to make restitution. Where there's real life (not just breathing life), there's hope—hope for victory, hope for at least some measure of restoration, hope for a fresh start. We shouldn't complain that it's only an opportunity and grumble that God won't make people love us and trust us.

Even the opportunity is more than we deserve.

Taking Time

If you're thinking, *Wow! This seems like a long process!* you're right.

With regard to sin *in general,* we're encouraged by God to enter a program of seeing it, hating it, and ferreting it out. Our mission is to understand the breadth and depth of our sin and to see it washed out where possible and cut out where necessary. God calls us to be perfect. If we could see how far from perfect we are, we wouldn't mind admitting that a long process is needed—a lifelong process with eternal consequences.

For any *particular* sin, though, we don't have to "wind down," commit it a little less each day, or have it linger for months or years. If we have the Holy Spirit, we have "everything we need for life and godliness."[7] We can run to Him every time and actually, really, truly never commit that sin again. Glory! I'm *not* a slave!

But being free not to sin doesn't mean that the evil desires will instantly disappear. It doesn't mean that the struggle will be easy. If we've gone deeply into a sin, if it's become a lifelong habit, we shouldn't think that we'll be able to defeat it easily. We never have to say yes to it again, but saying no may require a bloody war.

"In your struggle against sin, you have not yet resisted to the point of shedding your blood."[8] Make no mistake about it: Resisting sin is a struggle. It's warfare. Shedding our blood? Most of us would have to admit that we haven't even resisted to the point of shedding our *illusions.*

An important "battle" passage of the Bible is Ephesians 6, which deals with the armor of God and spiritual warfare. It's important to see the tools we have in this war. But it's all too easy to assume that the enemies are all "out there," outside of ourselves and the church—the "bad guys" in the visible world and the even "badder guys" in the demonic world.

But some of the fiercest warfare we ever face is against the enemy we carry inside—our own sinful nature. When war actually comes into our hearts, and the bullets are flying and the bombs are dropping and blood and tears are everywhere, we can be caught unprepared. We can say, "I didn't know God meant *war.*"

We should be ready to resist sin to the point of shedding our blood. This puts sin in a different perspective. If someone comes to us and says, "Sin, or I'll kill you," we should be willing to say, "Go ahead and kill me, because I'm not going to sin." "Let no sin rule over me," the psalmist prayed.[9] This is the calling that Christ has given us. And with His mighty help, we can do it.

We can stop.

FIFTEEN

They asked, "Lord, do you want us to call down fire from heaven to destroy them?" But Jesus turned and rebuked them.
Luke 9:54–55

God's Reluctance to Punish

God strikes with his finger, and not with all his arm.

George Herbert

And the man, falling on his knees, said to Jesus, 'Lord, please show mercy to me, a sinner.'"

"And Jesus said to him, 'You dirty, rotten, filthy, stinking bum! Get out of my sight!'"

The above "passage," of course, never happened. Jesus never treated people that way. One of the "hallelujah!" things about our God is that He's reluctant to punish. Unlike many "religious" people, He's unwilling to apply more heat than necessary.

God's patience doesn't mean we're free to sin. We can try to take advantage of His kindness by figuring that it gives us "room" to play with sin and wrong attitudes. God is "gracious and compassionate, slow to anger and abounding in love,"[1] but this shouldn't lead us to conclude that He's a fool.

Instead, His mercy should persuade us that we are blessed beyond hope. He is both holier and more gracious than we are. He hates sin but somehow finds a way to hold back His punishment because of His mercy and great love. This combination is exactly what we would hope to find in a perfect Father's heart.

We're told, in fact, that we shouldn't "show contempt for the riches of his kindness, tolerance and patience," because His "kindness leads [us] towards repentance."[2] Long before God begins punishing us, and long after we've deserved it, God uses kindness, tolerance, and patience—in short, mercy—to win us over.

Taking No Pleasure

The Lord says clearly, "I take no pleasure in the death of the wicked" (Ezek. 33:11). He may have to put the wicked to death, but doing so doesn't bring Him pleasure. The justice is pleasing to Him, but not the execution. He didn't create that person in His image and likeness just to destroy him. There are "objects of his wrath—prepared for destruction,"[3] but they weren't "prepared" for destruction from eternity without having any choice in the matter. By their own wicked decisions those people have driven God to take this measure, but that was never His preference.

The woman of Tekoa understood this. She rebuked David for banishing his son and said that God "devises ways so that a banished person may not remain estranged from him."[4] This is so very, very important. God doesn't want to "blast" us but rather is constantly making up ways to bring us back to Him. He rejoices when the wicked come back to their senses and "take hold of the life that is truly life"[5] as the prodigal son did. Our Abba wants to run up the road to meet them and treat them to the grandest of feasts.

Jonah had the opposite attitude. He refused at first to preach in Nineveh precisely because he knew that God was gracious and compassionate. Jonah wanted the Ninevites to be destroyed. He was afraid that they would repent after being confronted with their sins, which would allow God to hold back His punishing hand.

When what Jonah "feared" actually happened and all the citizens of Ninevah repented, Jonah complained bitterly. He accused God of being too soft and tender and said with anger, "I *knew* that you are . . . a God who relents from sending calamity."[6] Jonah wanted to take pleasure in the death of the wicked. He didn't understand that he was serving a God who had quite a different attitude.

Jonah missed God's heart by a thousand miles. Our great God is *very reluctant to punish us as we deserve.*

Better Treatment

"'What has happened to us is a result of our evil deeds and our great guilt, and yet, our God, you have punished us less than our sins have deserved and have given us a remnant like this'" (Ezra 9:13).

Praise God that He "does not treat us as our sins deserve!"[7] If our sins of thought, word, and action were punished line item by line item, we'd spend all of our days under the wrathful hand of God. All joy would be gone, all hope would be lost, and we would give in to despair.

But somehow God, in all His lofty majesty and holiness, doesn't treat us as our sins deserve, even though they deserve to get it good and hard. Our God takes His time, controls His reaction, keeps offering love. "The Lord is not slow in keeping his promise, as some understand slowness. He is patient with you, not wanting anyone to perish, but everyone to come to repentance."[8]

God does store up wrath for the day of judgment, and we can become a "storehouse" of His wrath. But, hallelujah, our Father resists pouring it out on us.

Mercy is so important in human interaction as well. Debbie once did something that, after she'd thought about it, she was sure would be a great offense to Beth. Debbie asked for a time to meet together and came to the meeting with great fear and trembling. They talked about other things for awhile, and then Debbie finally came to the subject that had been causing her such anxiety.

But before she said anything about the particular issue, she told Beth that she was so sure that she was wrong, so sure that she deserved to be the recipient of Beth's anger, that she wanted to throw herself on Beth's mercy—and was willing to get on her knees and beg for forgiveness. Beth responded as God so often and in so many ways responds to us: She told Debbie that she understood what she'd done, that it was forgiven, and that there wasn't any anger or wrath stored up toward her in her heart. The joy in Debbie's face was a sight to behold.

When we understand this truth about our God—that He's not holding something against us—the joy in our faces will also be a sight to behold.

Punishment and God's Reputation

God's name and reputation are very important to Him, as they should be to us. He doesn't want to be slandered by people who will all too easily rage against Him and accuse Him of being harsh.

This is why He tells us, "For my own name's sake I delay my wrath" (Isa. 48:9). Although God has every right to discharge punishment whenever an offense occurs, He often chooses to wait in order not to let His name be besmirched by any "cheap shots."

God's concern for His reputation is so strong that it's biblical to appeal to Him to delay His wrath on this very basis. After the incident with the golden calf, God was ready to destroy the children of Israel who were following (or generally not following) Moses. God told Moses that He was weary of the people and would give Moses a fresh start with a new and (hopefully) better batch of folks (an offer many leaders might consider taking!).

Moses' pleading is very instructive. He appealed to God on the basis of God's own name and reputation. "'Why should the Egyptians say, "It was with evil intent that [God] brought them out, to kill them in the mountains and to wipe them off the face of the earth"'?"[9] Moses admitted that the people were stiff-necked, but he suggested that God's gracious nature was on the line and that this should prevent Him from obliterating these floundering followers.

This concept is stunning. This excahnge with Moses shows us that God's very goodness is a restraining factor on His punishment. It also tells us that the world looks at Christians as people who are "tied in" with God, and that God's credibility is tied up with His treatment of His followers. Incredibly, God cooperates with this idea and agrees to restrain His punishment and wrath for the sake of His own reputation.

We're God's family. He's our Father and we're His children if His Holy Spirit is in our hearts. He'll punish us if we truly need it *because* He loves us and wants us to be on the right path. He also wants justice to be done. However, just as a good human father agonizes over the need to continually (and perhaps even severely) punish his children, so God agonizes over the need to punish us.

By no means should we feel free to sin because of God's good heart and His desire to protect His own name. It doesn't provide a defense for ongoing bad behavior.

But we should take advantage of God's patience without "taking advantage" of it.

Negotiating Restraint

One of the most incredible stories of the Bible occurs in relation to the horrifyingly bad city of Sodom.

God checks out Sodom and determines that it's time for it to be punished with consuming fire. God is always willing to tell His servants His plans: "[He] takes the upright into his confidence." "Surely the Sovereign LORD does *nothing* without revealing his plan to his servants the prophets."[10] He decides to confide His intentions to Abraham.

Abraham then becomes a negotiator *par excellence*. He starts by asking the Lord, based on the Lord's own commitment to justice, to spare this large and wicked city if at least fifty righteous people can be found in it. "Far be it from you to do such a thing—to kill the righteous with the wicked, treating the righteous and the wicked alike. Far be it from you! Will not the Judge of all the earth do right?"[11]

Abraham's comments can sound smart-alecky to our untrained ears, but God doesn't think so and agrees to the deal. Then, in an incredible exchange, Abraham presses the point. What about forty? The Lord agrees to withhold punishment for forty. Well then, how about thirty? All right. Then let's go further: What about twenty? Yes, for twenty. Finally, in a bold last push, Abraham gets the Lord to agree to withhold punishment if He can find just ten righteous people in the entire city.

The fact that ten righteous people couldn't be found doesn't void the importance of the "negotiation" part of the story. What does this mean? It means that we as friends and followers of God have a right to "negotiate" on behalf of our cities, communities, neighborhoods, and relationships. We can plead. We can haggle. We can press. We can ask God to hold back His overall punishment for the sake of the remnant, the righteous few. *We can influence God.*

In fact, we *should* do it. We should go boldly into the throne room on behalf of the people around us to negotiate and plead with God to hold back the punishment that can be so dreadful and severe. This is the godly *opposite* of rejoicing when conditions around us get worse and worse because it proves that the world is a rotten place or that the end of the world is near. We can be bold on behalf of mercy. Just as Abraham wasn't rebuked in the slightest for his boldness, neither will we be.

Jesus teaches this principle in the parable of the wheat and the tares. In this story, the wheat and the tares are allowed to grow together so that the punishment of the tares (wicked people) won't spill over onto the wheat (God's children). God has given us the opportunity to exercise effective intercession in His presence as we speak up for others who, like us, don't deserve his mercy.

Absolutely breathtaking.

This does *not* mean that we shouldn't long for justice to be done or pray against God's enemies. It does *not* mean that we should ask God to withhold His hand from judging hardened sinners who show no sign of ever repenting. Abraham's motivation wasn't to keep Sodom from being judged, but to keep the righteous (like Lot) from being destroyed. And God granted Abraham his desire (Lot was saved), even though the outward form of deliverance looked different than Abraham had imagined. Ultimately God won't spare a wicked civilization like Sodom—but He will spare the righteous who live there.

We should warn what's left of our civilization of this somber reality, even as we negotiate for mercy.

—————

What about pleading for ourselves?

We can cry out, "Correct me, LORD, but only with justice—not in your anger, lest you reduce me to nothing."[12] As we pray this prayer, we're acknowledging that we need to be rebuked or corrected, but we ask God not to do it in anger.

If we have sinned greatly, our first pleadings may seem to be denied—as they were in Jepthah's days. But the Israelites persisted in crying out, and God "could bear Israel's misery no longer."[13] What an encouragement to plead. Our Father can't bear our misery. He's with us. He understands.

If we don't feel that God is our true Father, we'll have a hard time pleading with faith and confidence. We'll either not pray at all or we'll do so with the haunting feeling that we have no right to ask for this, that we deserve whatever is coming at us down the road.

But if we know for sure that God is our Father, our Abba, then we'll believe that—even if we've been wrong—we can still plead for mercy. One of the awesome truths of Scripture is that the One from whom all punishment ultimately comes is also the source of an ocean of mercy.

"Remember not the sins of my youth and my rebellious ways."[14] We don't make this plea so we can continue in those sins, because a hardened persistence in sin can finally exhaust His mercy. But as long as we're still wrestling with God, we can expect to receive His bountiful mercy. He's our Father. We can *count* on His mercy.

Each of us has been "sinful from the time my mother conceived me."[15] Our lives have at times reeked of the stench of sin. We can find ourselves acknowledging God's supremacy even as our hearts struggle against obedience and rebel against His order. In all of this, we can—we should—we must—plead with our God to show mercy, to hold back His punishment.

And somehow, some way, to smile on us again.

∽

Part Four

Walking in Victory

SIXTEEN

Teach my people the difference between the holy and the common . . . the unclean and the clean.
Ezekiel 44:23

Learning the Difference between Discipline and Punishment

From the errors of others a wise man corrects his own.

Publilius Syrus

---

*L*ife is full of both discipline and punishment, and sometimes the two can seem strangely intermingled. Yet as we have seen, they are two very distinct paths. "The Lord *disciplines* those he loves, and he *punishes* everyone he accepts as a son."

It is absolutely critical that we learn to differentiate between discipline and punishment, because the purpose and the correct response to each one are opposites.

God disciplines us to make us stronger. He allows trials to come into our lives so that we can become "mature and complete, not lacking anything."[1] When we're disciplined, it's *not* because we've done something wrong, but because God wants us to grow up. Discipline says, "I'll make things hard for you because I love you."

What should we do as that discipline gets tougher and tougher and tougher? Should we stop and change our course? No! Discipline doesn't come because we've sinned, so it doesn't tell us that we need to stop doing something.

Instead, it comes to make us stronger. The only way it can do this is if we cry out to God and ask Him to help us persevere with wisdom through the trial.

Punishment, on the other hand, comes because we've sinned. It's designed to shake us off the wrong path and lead us back to the road that leads to life. Discipline can come even when we're doing the right thing, but punishment comes only when we're doing what's wrong.

If we're being punished, what should we do? Persevere? Continue? No! We're on the wrong path! We need to repent of our sin, turn off that wrong path, and return to the way that God has laid out for us.

The key question when we encounter trouble is: "Am I being disciplined, or am I being punished?" This distinction requires wisdom to see, but (praise God!) He *guarantees* that He'll give us wisdom *generously* and without finding fault (which is very loving and gracious of Him, especially if we're being punished). The only requirement is that we believe, and not doubt at all, that we will receive it.

John never sought this wisdom. His view was that his employees were just one giant trial. He believed that no one but he was committed to the company, and he told them so. Few people took any initiative or offered ideas that differed from John's, which he took as further "proof" that he was being "tested" by everyone.

In reality, though, John was being *punished* for his arrogance and abusive treatment of people. He enjoyed insulting his employees in public and tearing down those who were weak. He ridiculed any new ideas except his own. The result? His employees hated him and talked behind his back. They celebrated whenever he was out of the office. The day John dies, there'll be widespread happiness: "When the wicked perish, there are shouts of joy."[2]

How Will We Learn the Difference?

So how will we discern whether we're tasting discipline or punishment, God's refining or punishing fire?

Will it be by experience? We could take a survey of Christians and try to discern from their stories what God is "up to" in this pivotal business. This is, in fact, what many writers have done, deriving their theology from the waves of the public opinion sea. "Empirical research" they call it.

The key questions in this kind of survey never get asked: Are those surveyed responding according to the Spirit or the sinful nature? According to the Bible or their feelings? With a heart of flesh or a heart of stone? If there's a mix, or if we just don't know, then the "survey" is totally invalid from the only perspective that counts—God's.

And why would we want to base our lives on the opinions of people we don't even know anyway? Popularity and mass appeal are more often marks of a lie, or at least of something superficial, than they are of the truth.

There's a better way.

Because God has revealed Himself in the Scriptures, we need to look intensely into the Bible for our answers.

As we do, we'll look first at someone being disciplined, although his friends thought he was being punished. Then we'll look at someone being punished, although his friends thought he was being disciplined.

Who, while being disciplined, was accused—relentlessly—of being punished?

Job. Job was without peer, "blameless and upright, a man who fears God and shuns evil."[3] Trials of many kinds overwhelmed him, but it's clear from the Scriptures that they had *nothing to do with punishment*. He was in a test so incomprehensible that it makes most of our trials look puny by comparison. Even after problems unimaginable rained down upon him, he refused to curse God, who continued to brag about Job to Satan.

And consider Job's three friends. It's easy just to write them off—but look what they did: They went to "sympathize with him and comfort him. . . . they began to weep aloud, and they tore their robes and sprinkled dust on their heads." These men knew how to "weep with those who weep." Few of us have ever seen or felt their level of love and commitment, as "they sat on the ground with him *for seven days and seven nights.*"[4] They hadn't come to lecture him or tear him down. They had come to love him.

So what went wrong? What produced the agonizing conversations that fill most of the Book of Job? What do these three say that leads God to tell them, "I am angry with you . . . because you have not spoken of me what is right. . . . My servant Job will pray for you, and I will accept his prayer and not deal with you according to your folly"?[5] How had their love ended up in such an awful place as *folly*?

The answer? Their intentions started out all right, but they were confused about the difference between discipline and punishment. They mixed the two together in a way that made their advice deadly. Their love couldn't outweigh their ignorance of God and His ways. They became three of Job's "trials of many kinds."

As we read through the book of Job, their error becomes clear. It's not *what* they said that was wrong; on the contrary, we could pull out quotes from any of the three friends and have them stand as truths about our God: "Blessed is the man whom God corrects"; "If you put away the sin that is in your hand . . . you will lift up your face without shame"; "If you return to the Almighty, you will be restored."[6]

These statements are all true. The problem is that they were *misapplied*. They are true for anyone who is experiencing fire because of sin. But this wasn't the case with Job. His was a purifying fire, a refining fire, but not in any way a punishing fire. This was what his friends missed.

The difference between discipline and punishment is a matter of the heart, not of circumstances or of outward appearances.

And who was being punished, but thought that it was a trial from the Lord? No less a spiritual giant than Joshua.

The Israelites had just obliterated Jericho in a deliciously absurd way. A mighty city was reduced to nothing through marching and music and madness. God's power and their faith combined to win a shattering victory. God had given them only one boundary: don't touch the "devoted things," the things set apart for the Lord.

But Achan didn't obey. He took some of these things and hid them inside his tent, obviously with the knowledge and agreement of his family. The result was that the Israelites were soundly defeated by the little town of Ai.

And Joshua, of all people, missed it. "Ah, Sovereign LORD, why did you ever bring this people across the Jordan to deliver us into the hands of the Amorites to destroy us? If only we had been content to stay on the other side of the Jordan!"[7] What did he do? He blamed their defeat on the Lord. He accused God of bringing an unjust and totally disastrous trial onto His innocent people. A great man, one of only two who four decades before had wanted to go into the land, now tore his clothes and said that the discipline, the trials, and the pain were just too much.

But God didn't let Joshua go on in his confusion. "Stand up!" He commanded. "What are you doing down on your face? Israel has sinned. . . . That is why the Israelites cannot stand against their enemies . . . they have been made liable to destruction."[8] He told Joshua—and tells us—not to moan and groan and and blame God when it's our own sin that's causing a punishing fire. Instead, He told Joshua to search out the sin, deal with its cause, and get back on God's path.

If Joshua had refused to listen—if he had persisted in seeing punishment as discipline—he would have been left only with bad choices. He could have continued trying to fight a war while he had sin buried in the camp—which God makes clear would have led to annihilation. Or he could have stopped there—or even turned back—and the Israelites would have lost the Promised Land.

We don't want to miss this distinction in our own lives or the lives of those around us. To excuse fire as a discipline—perhaps even a confusing discipline, one of those "mysteries" of the Christian life—when it's really punishment is disastrous. It makes us "liable to destruction."

And if we don't see it clearly for what it is in the lives of those nearby and instead acquiesce by agreement or by silence in their wrong path, then we can get in on it and be punished too. Achan's family was executed with him. Sapphira followed Ananias to judgment and death.

But Abigail saw her husband Nabal's folly and impending doom clearly. She shines as one who saw punishment for what it was. She separated herself from Nabal's sin and thus avoided sharing in his punishment. She heard the report that David was coming with a small army against them and knew in her heart that David's coming was not a trial, not a discipline, not unjust suffering, but was instead a well-deserved judgment. She lived and was blessed, but Nabal remained a fool and was destroyed.

We can choose to see punishment as punishment and live as Joshua chose to do, or we can refuse to see God as a punisher and die like Achan. We can separate ourselves from one persisting in sin and live like Abigail, or we can cleave to the sinner and die like Sapphira. The decision is ours.

And how we make it is significant beyond description.

Steps to Discernment

How will we make the important distinction between discipline and punishment?

- We can ask God to show us the truth underlying the fires we're experiencing. We must ask Him to help us see why it hurts, why we're afraid, why we're confused, why we feel crushed. All suffering has a reason. We have to be open to the truth with ears to hear, however, and not defensively push it away.

- We can purpose to persevere through any trials-by-fire and to turn away from any punishments-by-fire.

- We can lay the facts as fully and honestly as we can before a wise person and ask for help in seeing the situation clearly. We have to resist "coloring" the details to make us look better or to get the answer we want. We have to allow him or her to probe us with uncomfortable questions. And we should write down all of their thoughts, even—especially—the ones we don't like.

- We can turn this book into an extended study. We can look up the Scriptures in the appendix after we've finished reading each chapter and let them sink in, slowly and deeply. As they pierce us, we can write down our thoughts right in this book or in a separate notebook. We can work to make these truths our own.

- We can look at the tie between the fire and its location. For example, problems in our work life can be either trials to prepare us for greater impact or punishments for being gossips or idlers. Because of the sow/reap principle of "natural consequences," we should start by looking for the answer to work-related fire in our work life (not home or church).

- We can avoid the superficial comments of others, who can all too easily encourage us when we need correction and correct us when we need encouragement. This includes comments from magazines, books, radio, and television. We need to remember that "advice" without intimate knowledge of the facts and the Scriptures might be worse than worthless.

- We can avoid superficial analysis of situations, the misleading attempts to quickly categorize things by "type." We can remember, for example, that a physical ailment can be a discipline (as it was for Job and the man born blind) or a punishment (as it was for the Egyptians and King Herod). We must look deeper to see what the underlying spiritual dimension really is.

Finally, we can begin—right now. We don't have to confuse discipline and punishment ever again.

On the next page are some important questions to ask ourselves to expose our hearts. On page 175 is a summary of some of the major ideas covered in this book.

Two other issues come into play: positive self-discipline and negative self-punishment.

Self-Discipline

Tony had been running his own home-based business for three months. He was excited about his ideas and goals and had written out a plan of action. But after working many years in the corporate world and having to arrive by a certain time, Tony was swallowed up by the freedom. He was enjoying "sleeping in" until he was ready to get up. He resisted even the idea of setting an alarm. Although he had accomplished some things during those three months, they were only half of what he had wanted to get done.

Tony learned an important lesson from the consequences (the missed opportunities, the growing frustration with his lack of accomplishment, the smaller bank account) of his

Questions to Ask

1. What area of my life is targeted by the fire?

2. Why is the fire coming *now*?

3. Do I need to change or simply persist in doing good?

4. What are my motives? What is my conscience telling me?

5. What hidden desires are being exposed?

6. Why do I want these things?

7. Why do they have such a powerful grip on me?

8. Where are these desires taking me?

9. How do I feel when I get there?

10. How are my motives and desires not in line with God and His Word?

11. What have I done to contribute to the problem?

12. Have I reviewed my situation with others? If not, am I willing?

undisciplined lifestyle. He learned that a small, regular "dose" of self-discipline can eliminate the more dramatic forms of discipline.

Paul didn't try to dodge discipline. Instead, he welcomed it. He looked for ways to "impose" discipline on himself. "I do not run like a man running aimlessly; I do not fight like a man beating the air. No, I beat my body and make it my slave so that after I have preached to others, I myself will not be disqualified for the prize" (1 Cor. 9:26–27).

Paul wasn't playing a game. He was in *strict* training. Why did he beat his body? Not because it was evil in itself, but because he knew that our bodies are a battleground in which the sinful nature (the "flesh") wars against our spirits. At its "best," the sinful nature yearns for sloppiness and disorder and builds bad habits into our physical lives. (At its worst, it drives us into the nether world of despair and the disintegration of our personalities.)

Learning the Difference

If fire comes into your life,
first discern if it is discipline or punishment

Meditate   List weaknesses   Review Scripture   Prioritize list   Study items   Write findings   Share with a friend

If

Discipline

Right Response:
1. Seek what it is in your life that God is honing
2. Adjust behavior if necessary and press on

Wrong Response:
1. Stop living for God
2. Avoid and deny pain
3. Grow weary/lose heart
4. Numb the pain
5. Make excuses for God
6. Grumble and complain
7. Blame God

Results:
A fuller and deeper relationship with the Lord, greater strength, more confidence

Results:
Sterner discipline, poverty and shame, death, lead others astray

Punishment

Right Response:
1. Repent (stop the wrong behavior)

Wrong Response:
1. Deny
2. Hide
3. Lose heart
4. Ignore
5. Justify
6. Compare
7. Become stiff-necked

Results:
Forgiveness, restored relationship with the Lord and others, a fuller life

Results:
Direct losses, loss of discernment, fear, shame and humiliation, separation, bitterness, rotting, judgment, wrath, consuming fire

Contrary to much teaching on the subject, the sinful nature *can't* be and *won't* be reformed. "The sinful mind is hostile to God. It does not submit to God's law, nor can it do so."[9] The sinful nature isn't what converted or changed when we became Christians. It *can't* be changed. It's a tyrant. Tyrants can't be reformed. They can only be killed.

When our spirits are revived by God, we begin to crucify this tyrant. We want to reclaim our bodies and offer them to God as weapons of righteousness. How do we do this?

- *Acknowledge.* The first step in crucifying the sinful nature is to clearly see that it exists. We can't defeat an enemy that we believe went away at our conversion. It will keep defeating us, even as our confusion leads us to think that our whole being is defective. The sinful nature is in us, but it isn't us. "It is no longer I myself who do it, but it is sin living in me."[10]

- *Anticipate.* Second, we have to believe that the sinful nature can be defeated. We're not "only a sinner, saved by grace." We're sons and daughters of the Living God. "This is the victory that has overcome the world, even our faith."[11] When people say, "Of course Christians will continue to sin," they're saying that the sinful nature can't be crucified, a deadly belief that isn't true.

- *Accept.* Third, we have to take up our cross daily. A cross has a purpose: something is supposed to be killed on it. That "something" is the sinful nature. We're involved in a blood-and-guts war. It goes on every day, rain or shine. Fall asleep just one day, and the enemy can get a foothold.

- *Abolish.* Fourth, we have to kill all of the "Canaanites." The Israelites were told that if they didn't, the survivors would be thorns in their eyes and sides. "Canaanites" inside of us—uncrucified things like anger, lust, greed, jealousy, gluttony—will, like the Canaanites of old, be thorns in our eyes and sides.

- *Acquire.* Fifth, we must crucify the sinful nature by acquiring Christ's power, not using our own puny efforts to be "better." We came by faith, and we must walk the same way.

We must, however, be determined to win. "A man is a slave to whatever has mastered him"[12] we are warned, "but I will not be mastered by anything." We don't have to be slaves. "It is for freedom that Christ has set us free." We're free. We can hear the emancipation proclamation; we can feel the chains slipping off; we're ready for the Year of Jubilee.

What so many of us want is to have a soft, easy life and still be mature Christians. Faced with the choice of one or the other, many Christians choose the easy life over the disciplined life, the civilian life over the military life. We choose to pamper our bodies instead of going into strict training. We're all too often spectators instead of participants.

At the end of our lives, it won't matter to us how much time we spent at the office, how many movies we watched, how many vacations we took, or how many acquaintances we had. It won't matter if there are five thousand people at our funeral or five. It will only matter that we won.

It will be glorious at the end of life to be able to say, "I *did* beat my body and make it my slave. I *did* endure hardship as a good soldier of Jesus Christ. I *have* fought the good fight, I *have* finished the race, I *have* kept the faith. Now there is in store for *me* the crown of righteousness, which the Lord, the righteous Judge, will award to me on that day."[13] What's the "prize"? It's hearing God say, "Well done, good and faithful servant." It's receiving the best reception, reputation, recognition, rewards, responsibilities, rest, and rejoicing that heaven can think up.

The only way we'll receive the crown of righteousness is if we submit to God's discipline in our lives and exercise self-discipline, so that after we've preached to others we ourselves "will not be disqualified for the prize."[14]

<u>*The Prize*</u>.

Self-Punishment

Since discipline means the training and honing of our lives to be more like Christ, we should consider it an ally and look for ways to fill our lives with it. With punishment, however, the opposite principle applies. *We are never called to punish ourselves.*

We can have two contradictory orientations toward punishment. The first is to do everything we can to avoid receiving just punishment for our actions. The other is to inflict ourselves with undue and unnecessary punishment. We hate what we deserve and welcome what we don't. This self-inflicted punishment is both unnecessary and destructive. It beats us down, steals our joy, and leaves our hearts ravaged by doubts and confusion.

God wants us to live "free." We can't be free if we're constantly burdened by the weight of self-inflicted punishment. Let's take a look at a few of the bad reasons we inflict punishment upon ourselves.

Leftover Guilt—Many people don't like leftovers. I enjoy them after a favorite meal (and before they start looking like a high school biology experiment). But every day, many people devour a leftover that is both bitter and distasteful: the leftover of clinging guilt.

Guilt can be an effective tool in the hands of God to bring our hearts to the point of repentance and true change. Leftover guilt, however, is destructive; and with God's help it must be rooted out of our life.

Leftover guilt is the lingering feeling, after we've repented of a sin and been forgiven by God, that we still deserve judgment. It's not the realization that we may face additional consequences for our actions: it is prudent to see this. Instead, it's an unseen, unclear, haunting feeling that pent-up anger from somewhere is about to be unleashed against us in disastrous—and possibly unfair—ways.

But God has a better idea. He forgives "the guilt of [our] sin."[15] Somehow, amazingly, He doesn't just forgive our sins; He forgives the *guilt* of our sins. What a gift!

False Guilt—We can also be strangled by guilt that's unrelated to anything that we've actually done. This guilt can be inflicted on us by experiences in our past, an angry person, an abusive environment, or an oppressive relationship. It's a performance-oriented guilt, which often operates through a misinformed and mis-trained conscience.

Jan had a heavy load of responsibility, including several children and a husband who criticized her if dinner wasn't perfectly prepared by exactly six o'clock. Hal, a man with many professional and family responsibilities, was berated by his elderly mother because he "only" visited her once a week. Mona, who was already overcommitted, continued to say "yes" at her church because any time she said "no" the pastor's wife questioned her "spirituality."

True guilt only comes when we've violated God's standards. But we can also feel guilty because we haven't lived up to somebody else's expectations. False guilt can riddle our hearts every day, related both to past failures and a fear of future ones. We fear that we'll never measure up to the other person's expectations—and indeed we likely never will.

We were put here to run a grand race, not to measure up to the petty demands of some self-inflated tyrant. Why should we live our lives in constant response to the demands of others, controlled by everyone, driven by false guilt, and feeling like dirt whenever our "performance" doesn't measure up? Enough! God didn't call us to live such a life.

Perfectionism—Some of the greatest perpetrators of self-punishment are the people we see in our own mirrors.

We can be driven by perfectionism, a performance-based orientation that motivates everything we think, say, and do. If we finish three excellent projects in a day but don't get a fourth one started, we feel like failures. Or we may complete two of them excellently and one satisfactorily; again, we feel inadequate because the third one wasn't perfect.

We're trying to convince ourselves, others, and possibly even God that we're worthy of love because we've earned it. But the drive is never successful. How perfect do we have to be to feel that God will accept us? Or that others will approve of us? Or that we can accept ourselves as something of value? In this system, we can never be good enough.

Perfectionism can show up in our habits, our projects, our relationships, even our housecleaning. It can come from a broken past that we're still trying to fix, insecurities that drive us to be in control, or fears that press us to avoid doing anything unless we can do it flawlessly.

The antidote includes knowing and doing the good works that God (not other voices from the past or present) wants us to do and not trying to do more. It means knowing that good enough is good enough. It contains a "permission" to ourselves to be less than superhuman.

We have to be careful about what we try to accomplish "during the few days of life God has given [us]."[16] Many "teachers," through television, radio, books, magazines, and seminars, are willing to burden us with a long list of the things we "must" do in order to live a "godly" life. Although these teachers *may* have good intentions, if we tried to do everything they all said, we'd be dead within a year.

As the years are rushing past, I am finally coming to the point where I can see at least some of the good works that God is calling me to do. But, I don't have time to teach several Sunday school classes, lead a men's group, share regularly and intimately with three or four friends, spend individual time with everyone in my family every day, fast several days a week, read through the entire Bible several times a year, homeschool all of my children regardless of their ages or academic needs, bake my own bread, be involved in every cause and issue, grow all of my own vegetables in my own garden, and set up a winepress to teach my children how to squeeze the grapes with their feet.

I haven't even mentioned not having the time to repair my own car (I don't even *want* to know how to do this anymore!), camp, memorize a thousand verses, do street corner evangelism, serve on the boards of several nonprofit organizations, attend every event planned by my church or my children's school, repair the plumbing, rewire the house, paint the exterior, do all the yard work, or attend every seminar that promises to make me a better husband, father, or friend.

I can't do all these things. I *won't* do all these things. Christ has set me free.

And I intend to stay that way.

The "Mix"

What if we're experiencing *both* fires at the same time? What if we're doing some things that warrant punishment and receiving some fiery trials all at once? In fact, what if we're experiencing both punishment and discipline in the same situation?

Our hearts can be a mix of good and evil, and so it's no wonder that we can be feeling the heat of both strands of God's fire simultaneously. Like a patient investigator, we can with God's help unravel the strands and see how much weight to apply to each one.

The priority is to make sure first that we're not facing God's consuming fire, punishment for sin. We've got to get out of danger before the full value of God's refining fire can even be felt. We need to take time before the Lord to be certain that we aren't losing more than we're gaining.

Then we're ready to go through the process of discovering what God might be doing in our lives with His refining fire, as He disciplines us to make us mature.

Life is more complex than it appears to be in our earlier years or more rigid phases. It isn't just a matter of making a decision about life at age twenty and then carrying it out without questions or challenges until age eighty. It's a long, slow, painstaking, and pain-causing process, more like the storms and waves that etch a shoreline than the warm water and foam that soothe us in a tub.

Can we really see the difference between discipline and punishment?

The answer is a strong "yes"—if we really want to. As with so many things, the choice is left with us. We can plow ahead without giving thought to our ways, without taking time to analyze the pain, without seeing where our path is taking us. Or we can decide to have a better life and see it from the viewpoint of a majestic celestial Being who for some almost unbelievable reason thinks we're special.

The wonderful news is that our Father *wants* us to be successful in this life-important process of discerning the difference.

And He'll help us—every step of the way.

SEVENTEEN

His father had never interfered with him by asking,
"Why do you behave as you do?"
1 Kings 1:6

Applying the Principles in Families

Juvenile delinquency starts in the highchair
and ends in the death chair.

James D. C. Murray

Sometimes it seems that most of the mistakes that can possibly be made in relationships are made in families. A home can be a wonderful place to love and be loved, help and be helped, encourage and be encouraged. It can also be the primary place where hearts are crushed or killed, useful discipline is avoided, and punishments are out of proportion to the "crime."

God has a clear plan to discipline and punish each of us, including our family members, as the need arises. Occasionally He deals with us directly, but often He uses other people. Are we willing to be used by God to carry out a portion of His plan in the lives of our family members? Have we thought clearly, for example, about what steps we should be taking to discipline and punish our children? On the other hand, we may not be the agent that God uses in particular cases. Are we willing not to intervene, and let our loved ones be disciplined or punished by God or someone else?

These are questions of great importance. Much discipline and punishment that needs to occur with children is glossed over or not done at all. Much of what does occur is a confusing blend of the two.

Failing to distinguish between discipline and punishment can also cause us to unintentionally harm our spouses and other family members. We can intervene when they're being disciplined and keep them from growing to maturity. We can advise them to change directions when their rewards will be found just on the other side of the trial. Or, we can encourage them to persevere through a "trial" that is really a punishment. We can get in the "middle" of the punishment and end up confusing them and leaving them in their sin.

Or, we can do it well.

Applying the Principles with Children

Just as the starting point for understanding God as discipliner and punisher is understanding Him as Abba Father, so the starting point for understanding our parental role as discipliners and punishers is to see ourselves as loving abbas. God is a good Father. We need to treat our children the way He treats us. The most effective discipline and punishment take place when we have a deep relationship with our children that they don't want to see broken.

Being a good parent means we begin by "crawling inside our children's hearts."[1] This means we really come to know them—their unique perspectives, their interests and values, their strengths and weaknesses. This is key to discerning whether they need discipline or punishment. It's basic to getting the response we want from them.

The attitude we need goes something like this: "I love you and care about your life so very much. So much, in fact, that I'm willing to do things for you that won't be pleasant for either of us. I'll help you if the load gets too heavy, but I'm going to let you be tried by the challenges of life and learn by doing. I'm going to resist the temptation to bail you out when things get tough. If you're wrong—if you break the few clear rules we have in this home—and refuse to change, I'll punish you to get your attention. I'd rather spend my time thinking up blessings, but because I love you I'll punish you if you force me to do it."

Love and discipline aren't opposites. Discipline isn't separate from love—it's a part and *proof* of love. We don't have to find the "balance" between love and discipline, as though they were two ideas at odds with each other. Love expresses itself in discipline. Discipline is one of the voices of love. If we think discipline is a departure from love, then our discipline (and our punishment) of our children can either come to them without love or be erroneously cut back because we don't want to appear to be "unloving."

The goal of our discipline and punishment should be to *internalize* values in our children. It's so easy to externalize values—to do things that cause an "acceptable" outward appearance or behavior—while on the inside our children are seething with wrong ideas and evil desires. The question to ask about our children is: "Is this discipline or punishment going to help them develop self-control, so they can learn to 'watch' themselves?"

Discipline

Too many parents, when discipline is appropriate, punish instead. We see our children's fumblings and imperfections and want to "drive" those things out of them. Instead of carefully training them, we become angry and punish them. Our failure to control ourselves turns our discipline into punishment—perhaps even harsh punishment.

But another reason we punish when we should discipline is because we don't distinguish between the two. We discipline our children so they'll be "good steel." The issues involved aren't sins, but things that will hinder them in their spiritual race—things that in some cases could turn into sins if not redirected early on. The disciplines that we bring or allow into their lives are spiritual exercises and training. These disciplines can be—sometimes *should* be—very strong.

When children spill a drink or don't cooperate with potty training or get their "nice" clothes dirty or leave their room a mess, it's easy to go into "punishment mode" and deal with those actions as though they were sins.

But often they aren't. A lot of life is simply imperfect. If we attack the imperfection as "rebellion," using strong words and punishments, the results can be disastrous. On the other hand, if we carefully train our children, we can help help them mature without destroying their hearts.

Jessica was an intelligent seven-year-old whose bedroom was always a total disaster. She was a "pack rat" and seemed to enjoy living in the midst of disorder. Her parents established some reasonable standards, which Jessica didn't follow. They chose to first look at the situation as a need for discipline (almost always a good first assumption). So they bought her plastic organizing containers and showed her how to use them. When she still didn't respond, they increased the fire of discipline by the use of consequences: anything not put away went to their room for a time—a long time if necessary.

Disciplines can be "of many kinds." They can be relatively easy, like requiring our children to write thank-you notes after they've opened a present but *before* they begin playing with it. Or they can be hard, like requiring a child who consistently overcommits to stay up and work until 4:00 A.M. to accomplish what they've agreed to do.

If we really love our children, we discipline them. We let them go through challenges, even strong challenges. We don't pray that their life will be "easy" because we want them to become mature and complete. We let them do what they're capable of doing, even if we could do it more easily. We permit them to experience the consequences of their actions so they can learn truth and lessons deeply.

Sometimes life expects a lot and throws a lot of things at us at once. We should prepare our children for real life by inserting and allowing some disciplines into their childhood, so they'll know how they should live and respond.

Punishment

Punishment, on the other hand, is a response to sin and is designed to get our children off the wrong path and back onto the right one. Used properly, it can be very effective. Used improperly, it can be very destructive.

In Jessica's case, the discipline brought some improvement, but her parents were now able to see that there was also an element of rebellion in her response. They told her that any day her room was in disarray she would go to bed early with no reading, listening to tapes, or snacks. The next day she used the "solution" of locking her room instead of cleaning up. The rebel was unbowed. Her parents stepped up the punishing fire by taking away even more privileges. When Jessica saw the price she would have to pay for her poor choice of solutions, she finally chose to stop going in what had become a very painful direction.

Children aren't born "good." Although they were created in the image of God, they also carry the scars of the Fall. At a very young age, they can become convinced that they're the center of the universe.

When someone thinks that he's the center of the universe, how does he start to act? Like he *is* the center of the universe! The number one goal of his life is to get what's "coming" to him and to generally have his own way.

What do we have to do with our children to work that self-centered unpleasantness out of them? We have to punish them. If we don't, the sin-cancer in them will grow, and they'll bring us and themselves such grief when they're older that the little "grief" they missed along the way will seem like nothing by comparison.

Punishment can be "underdone." Too often we parents excuse the sin in our children's lives by saying that the child is too young to know better or that she's "tired" or "sick" or "going through a stage." Or we can be afraid to deal with it because we don't want to be "critical" or make her feel "bad" about herself or drive her away from us. So we try to nag the sin to death (which is neither appropriate nor effective). Or we punish only until we begin to feel "uncomfortable" and then stop the punishment before our children stop the sinning.

Punishment can also be "overdone." Children can't be and shouldn't be "beaten into submission." We should always keep in mind that God doesn't treat us as *our* sins deserve. If we give every sin the maximum punishment—and every imperfection that really needs discipline the maximum punishment—we'll crush the spirits of our children and shut the doors of their hearts to us. We should follow the rule of Rene Descartes: "A state is better governed which has but few laws, and those laws strictly observed."

What are some questions we could ask ourselves to see if our punishment of our children is underdone or overdone?

Underdone:

- Am I listening to my children's excuses for bad behavior?
- Am I *making* excuses for my children's bad behavior?
- Am I afraid of my children's reaction when I punish them?
- Am I concerned about my children's withdrawal of affection when I punish them?
- Am I nagging their behavior rather than taking steps to correct it?
- Have I seen any actual improvement in their attitude or behavior?

Overdone:

- Have I carefully taught my children what's right and what isn't?
- Am I punishing only for violations of God's standards and for open rebellion?
- Do I have a lot of rules?
- Is punishment a common, ongoing part of our life?
- Are my punishments excessive? (It may help to ask others this question.)
- Are my children's demeanors beaten down and lifeless when they're around me?

We need to punish our children, but we must do so *reluctantly,* just as God punishes us. Punishment should be used rarely or, like anything that's overused, it'll lose its value. Studies have shown that people are remarkably adaptable in situations of unremitting punishment and fear—they learn how to cope with the stress without making the necessary changes in attitude. They do only what they need to do to avoid stirring up a tyrant's wrath.

Additionally, punishment must be combined with "crawling" inside our children's hearts. We need to probe to find out what the root of the sin is. While we're doing it, we should acknowledge—to ourselves and to them—that we've faced similar temptations. Always, we need to remind them that they're still loved.

God doesn't excuse any sin, and He's given us the responsibility to work with Him to weed it out of our children's lives. Eli the priest received one of the strongest punishments anywhere in Scripture because he knew about his sons' sins yet "failed to restrain them." God said He "would judge his family forever."[2] David is likewise rebuked because he never interfered with his son Adonijah by asking him why he behaved the way he did.[3]

Jesus was very clear that His truth and His very presence would *divide* families. He expects us not to let sentiment rule over our love for Him. He expects us to love our children enough not to let them be fools. Truth, not "comfortable" relations, is the standard He uses. Few parents understand how important this is.

Those who do can achieve great things with their families.

When Discipline and Punishment Become Confused

How do we know whether a child should be disciplined or punished? The best way is to watch what he says and does. "Even a child is known by his actions, by whether his conduct is pure and right."[4] Childish ignorance or carelessness calls for discipline not punishment. But a child who stomps his foot and screams "no" at you is exhibiting hard-core rebellion—and that demands punishment.

Here are some examples of behaviors that probably require discipline and some others that probably require punishment.

Discipline

Action	Possible Response
Poor table manners	One-on-one private training
Not getting homework done	Don't send an excuse to school
Not getting chores done	More chores and loss of privileges
Not saving money	They miss what they can't afford
Being late	Start the activity or go to the event without them

Punishment

Action	Possible Response
Open rebellion (young child)	Time-out or moderate spanking
Open rebellion (older child)	Grounding
Lying about a sibling	Give them the punishment they were trying to get for the other
Stealing	Give a favorite toy away
Complaining	Give them more of what they are complaining about

What happens if we make a mistake and discipline when we should have punished or punish when we should have disciplined?

If a child is disciplined when he should be punished, he'll learn to disregard sin or treat it lightly. He'll learn that he can continue his sinful attitude if he disguises his outward behavior and jumps through some rule "hoops." These rules "lack any value in restraining sensual indulgence," [5] but they can give us false confidence that sin is being dealt with.

If Billy punches Susan, for example, he needs to be punished. He shouldn't just be required to say, "I'm sorry," and be given some additional chores to "keep him busy." If we've made this mistake, we need to go back to Billy's attitude, his core violence, and punish it appropriately.

If a child is punished when she should be disciplined, on the other hand, she'll become bitter and resentful. She'll learn that her parents are not just. She'll probably transfer that attitude to God and assume that God will punish her randomly and unjustly, too.

If, for example, our children start arguing or fighting, we need to determine who's at fault and not just send everyone to their rooms or spank them all. If we've made this mistake, we need to go back to our children with humility and genuine remorse and ask for forgiveness.

Inscribed on a little placard in the back of the Saint Louis Cathedral is a warning to King Louis IX of France (after whom the cathedral is named) from his mother. She told him that she would rather see him dead at her feet than have him offend Almighty God.

Would we like to see our children dead at our feet? Absolutely not! That would totally break our hearts. But would we rather see them that way than have them be a stench in the nostrils of God? If God is first in our lives, the answer would have to be "yes"—a reluctant yes, but a yes nonetheless.

Only if we have this attitude will we have the desire and courage to discipline them consistently when they need to be trained and to punish them carefully when they need to be stopped. And only if we do that can we ever raise them to be godly champions for Christ.

Applying the Principles with Spouses and Other Family Members

When our spouses and other family members face God's fire, our first response should be to observe and discern what's behind their struggles. Then, if we see that they're being disciplined, we should be encouragers, helpers, and fellow sufferers. If, on the other hand, they're being punished, we must be instructors, dissuaders, and possibly withdrawers.

One of the basic truths of life is that God is always "up to something" in the lives of our family members. The key for us is to watch their lives closely, not to "nitpick" but to observe the overall direction and the steadiness of each step. Then we want to ask God for discernment so we can turn our observations into an honest and useful analysis that can guide our responses to them and their decisions.

We don't want to jump into their fiery times too soon, before we even know what they're about. We want to take the time to make sure that we've cast aside any illusions about who they are, to make sure that we've come to a balanced view of what's going on in their lives.

If we discern that God is disciplining them—through the loss of a job, an overwhelming list of demands at work, a teacher who is demanding or unreasonable, a car that quits working, a financial setback, an illness, the betrayal of a friend—we can help them in three ways.

- *Encourager.* We can help them "find strength in God."[6] We can exhort them to persevere, to never give up, to find "pure joy" in the midst of the test.

- *Helper.* We can also help them in their trial. We can "carry each other's burdens." We can give them that "lift" that energizes them into high gear. This doesn't mean that we do it all for them, "for each one should carry his own load."[7] So we work to find the balance, to know how much help is enough, to understand when it's time to let them do it alone.

- *Fellow Sufferer.* We can be a fellow sufferer. Since "no discipline seems pleasant at the time, but painful,"[8] we can sympathize and empathize with their pain. We can "mourn with those who mourn."[9] We can be like Job's friends, who loved him enough to sit with him and grieve for days. We want our loved ones to be able to say, "It was good of you to share in my troubles," and "just as you share in our sufferings, so also you share in our comfort."[10]

If, on the other hand, we discern punishment—perhaps in the very same list of circumstances mentioned above—we can move in three different roles.

- *Instructor.* We can become instructors about God's law and their response to this law that is causing them to be punished. *Great* care must be exercised not to "script" people—to give them a list of rules they can keep or an outward change they can masquerade while their hearts remain unchanged. Superficial change won't fool or satisfy God, and ultimately it won't satisfy us (even if it fools us for a while).

- *Dissuader.* Beyond instruction, we can become active dissuaders. We can plead with them to stop their sinful behavior. We can speak freely (but carefully) with other family members and friends, asking them to help us in our efforts and helping them to see through any masquerade. We can bring in spiritual authority, with (hopefully) its truth and warnings. And we can pray "imprecatorily"—strongly and pointedly—against their sin, asking God to bring them to their knees.

- *Withdrawer.* We can come to the point where we must withdraw from the one who persists in stony-heartedness and wooden-headedness. Biblically, we *should* withdraw from those who claim to be Christians but are living a sham. We can survive and be blessed like Abigail and not "go down with the ship" like Achan's wife or Sapphira. Nothing—not marriage or any other family relationship—requires us to share in the sins or punishments of another.

Discernment about what God's doing and what's really going on in the lives of others is the key, both in parenting and in other family relationships. In one sense discernment is easy to come by—for if we ask in faith God gives it to us "generously . . . without finding fault."[11] But in another sense it's very hard to come by—because we're imperfect and carry incorrect assumptions and others are imperfect but can masquerade quite effectively.

We must take the time and be courageous enough to find and face the truth. Only then will we know where others' hearts are. Only then will we know if they're being disciplined or punished. Only then will we know the proper response each step of the way. Only then will we be effective in our relationships.

Only then will we be like God.

EIGHTEEN

Two are better than one . . . if one falls down,
his friend can help him up.
Ecclesiastes 4:9–10

Applying the Principles with Friends and Acquaintances

The truth that is suppressed by friends
is the readiest weapon of the enemy.

Robert Louis Stevenson

To distinguish between discipline and punishment is difficult with our friends. It's almost impossible with acquaintances.

With family members, we have a "history." We've lived with them. We have an accumulation of facts—from direct observation, from conversations, from others' input whose lives relate closely to them. We often have a common heritage that explains many of the challenges and temptations of their lives. We have a "sense" about who they are and where they're going.

But with friends, except for the very rare friendship in which an intimate "family" relationship is formed, we have "missing pieces." We generally haven't lived with them. We don't spend enough time with them to really know any more about them than they want us to know at any given point in time. We're missing the heritage and the special "sense" about their lives' courses.

Friends can put up a bold front to keep us from seeing who they really are. There are very few of the one-spirit, David-and-Jonathan kind of friendships; and the farther a relationship moves away from this level of intimacy, the harder it will be for those involved to discern discipline and punishment in each other's lives.

And what about acquaintances? They range from people we've met and talked with, through people we've only observed and heard discussed by others, to people that we've read or heard about but never met. It's astonishing how many conclusions Christians are willing to draw about God and truth and life from situations that they know little or nothing about. In some cases, the reality of that situation may be the exact *opposite* of what it appears to be. Attempting to give advice to acquaintances can be absolutely disastrous.

In this chapter, we'll take a look at how to apply the principles of discipline and punishment to friendships. After that, we will discuss what to do—and not to do—with acquaintances.

Comforting the Afflicted

If our friends are under God's discipline, we want to encourage them to persevere through the trial.

Is there anything more beautiful, other than the Lord's own encouragement, than to have someone come alongside of us when we're facing trials and help us to carry the load? Paul asked his friends to "endure hardship *with us*."[1]

I told a dear friend once (make sure you explain what you've learned about discipline before you say these things!), "I know that you're in a lot of pain right now. I know that you're undergoing a fiery trial and that it hurts. If I could push a button and make the pain go away, one part of me would do it. But there's another part of me, a deeper part, a spirit part, that's praising God you're going through this! You'll be made a more beautiful and better person, you'll have glory revealed in you, and you'll have these very troubles achieve the 'eternal glory that far outweighs them all.'"[2]

We do *not* want to pray away all suffering from those we love. Instead, we should pray that the eyes of their hearts will be opened, so that they can see what that suffering is achieving for them and how much greater the glory will be than the pain is now. In fact, the glory *far* outweighs all the pain.

What if someone we know, for example, is sick? The friend whose sickness is a trial needs our love, our encouragement, and our prayers. They need to know that God is both able and willing to heal them. They need to know that we're going to stick with them.

Abraham and Isaac walked through a trial together. God told Abraham to sacrifice his son, and Isaac eventually understood that he was the sacrifice. But their hearts were wrapped up together. Astonishingly, neither of them ever complained. Abraham didn't struggle against God, and Isaac didn't struggle against Abraham. They faced this discipline, the most fiery of trials, together. Their victory in perseverance was so great that they became our fathers in the faith—for faith is always required to persevere through a trial.

Faith is based on the knowledge that God our Father is both good and trustworthy. It's *not* an irrational "just trust in the Lord" when you're really expecting to lose. Faith is having the confidence in God that any trial will be for our good and that *all* trials will end in victory if we persevere and don't "shrink back."[3]

Trials are the testing ground of individual hearts, but also of friendships. "A brother is born for adversity," we're told.[4] This doesn't mean they were put here to *cause* adversity! Rather, at the very deepest level, a friend is there to help bear us through the almost unbearable times. In a very real way, our trial becomes their trial. They encourage us, help us, bleed with us, die with us.

Perhaps the greatest trial of all would be to face death for a friend. That's the moment when friendship and love are defined at their most glorious level: "Greater love has no one than this, that he lay down his life for his friends."[5] There is no greater trial.

And no greater love.

Afflicting the Comfortable

If our friends are in great pain because God is punishing them, we can go to them and do something that we are scripturally forbidden to do: go to these (at least partly) hardhearted and hardheaded persons with sympathy.

Many think that this is the "Christian" way, perhaps because they don't understand that Christians can be punished or they don't think they should "judge." If we show sympathy to a person being punished, we can get "between" him and God and muddy the issues. "Encouragement" in this situation is in reality a great lie.

Why would we want to think that others (at least everyone but our enemies) are doing better than they really are? Perhaps because if we acknowledge the problems in their lives, we'll have to admit to the same problems in our own lives. Perhaps we want to avoid confrontation. Maybe it's just easier to pretend and carry on superficial relationships. And people can wield the "do not judge" verses as a sword to keep that painful "enemy"—truth—at a distance. But wishing won't make others better than they really are. Instead, it helps to keep them trapped in their sinful ways.

What we should do instead is go to our friends when God is punishing them and help them to see that they're on the wrong path. We need to let God's fire burn from our hearts into their lives.

"Better is open rebuke than hidden love. Wounds from a friend can be trusted."[6] Many people think that a true friend is one who never rebukes or wounds. They think their friends should just "accept them the way they are" and let them "be." Let them be what? A fool? A person headed for destruction? Whatever such acceptance is, it's not love.

A true friend is one who's willing to wound us with her rebuke. She loves us too much not to help us see our blind spots. She sees the powerful people God wants us to be and the blessings which God longs to heap upon us, and she'll do all she can, including bringing us a strong rebuke, to help us achieve those things.

But the wounds of a friend are always *faithful*. That's why we can trust them. A friend doesn't blast away at our lives and hearts with recklessness and joy. She doesn't come with arrogance and disdain. She doesn't rub it in. She doesn't come with conclusions and only pieces of information.

Instead, a friend comes in humility and the fear of the Lord, knowing that she brings a fire which will wound our hearts, but loving us too much not to bring it. She gets our input and adjusts her message accordingly. And when she gives the message, she's grieved for us and with us. She understands our humanness, our neediness, the lure and power of temptation, the difficulty of seeing sin clearly. She understands the meaning of the question, "Who is led into sin, and I do not inwardly burn?"[7] She hurts when we hurt and bleeds with us and for us. No gossip or slander here.

And with the rebuke, a true friend brings comfort—not a comfort that encourages a sin to continue, but a comfort that says, "I'm with you." I've had people say to me, "You're the very person who showed me the Scriptures that pierced my heart, but now I'm back asking you for comfort." How can it be that the person who wounds us is the same one who comforts us? It seems so contradictory.

Yet God treats us with both strength and softness, and He calls us to have both of these in balance in our relationships with each other. A friend is someone who's willing to rebuke but then holds the one rebuked. He brings a powerful admonition but then cries with the one admonished. And, like God, he walks along with his friend back to the right path that leads to life and blessing.

Earlier we talked about praying for the healing of someone whose sickness is a result of discipline. The reverse would be true here. How easy it can be to begin praying uncritically for the healing of one of our friends! But what if his sickness is a punishment?

If he doesn't repent and confess his sin, no amount of praying on our part can guarantee a healing. Healing is tied in Scripture to confession and forgiveness. But our undiscerning prayer, when it goes unanswered, can damage our faith. It can leave us wondering about God's goodness or the effectiveness of prayer, when we've actually brought this crisis on ourselves by not knowing the other as deeply as we should and not discerning what God is doing in his life.

The answer? We must be good physicians. We need to diagnose before we prescribe. If it's sin, we must call it so. Then, as discussed in detail in the last chapter, we must instruct, and dissuade, and if necessary withdraw. We must not make the fatal error of calling punishment a "trial" or offering "peace . . . when there is no peace." We must "let God be true, and every man a liar."[8]

If you do this, "you will save both yourself and your hearers."[9]

Dealing with Acquaintances

An acquaintance is someone whom we know only at a distance. Perhaps we hardly know him at all. This is a dangerous ground with regard to discipline and punishment.

The problem is that we know little or nothing on which to base our thoughts, our prayers, or our actions. Our response must be careful and measured. We don't want to leave anything undone that's one of the "good works" that God has designed for us to do. But we also don't want to get ahead of the Spirit, and we never, ever want to move opposite to Him.

At the first level is someone who needs immediate physical help. The good Samaritan didn't take time to try to discern whether the beaten man was being disciplined or punished. We don't need to hesitate before we stop to help a stranded motorist or someone choking to death in a restaurant. We want to be neighbors, good neighbors. Jesus' instruction was clear: "Go and do likewise."[10]

The next level includes physical needs which aren't so acute or spiritual or emotional needs described to us by the acquaintance or someone who "knows" him. Here the *real* need isn't so immediate or even obvious. Before we dispense advice or help, we need to know more so that our advice will be accurate and our help will really be helpful. Before we pray, we need to have more background, or else pray with "conditions" ("if this, then God please do that"). If we don't know enough to pray, perhaps we shouldn't pray at all.

Ignorance is no excuse for confusing discipline and punishment or for helping to confirm someone else in their confusion. Christianity abounds with shallow relationships. Many people act like the most fleeting encounter or minimal contact gives them all manner of "insight" and excuse to talk about or direct the lives of others.

Many Christians, for example, really like "prayer chains." At their worst they can become "gossip chains," but even at their best they're often very much amiss. The theory behind prayer chains seems to be that the more people we can get praying for us, the better. But God has never been interested in numbers. Will their prayers help us if they're out of fellowship with God and "even [their] prayers are detestable"?[11] Will our prayers help them if we're praying opposite to their real needs or the direction of their lives?

We've explored how difficult it is to pray properly even for friends when they're sick. How much more of a problem it is when we're asked to pray for total strangers! We could be praying for the healing of a murderer or rapist, when God is using their sickness as both a punishment and a way of keeping them from doing further harm.

Will God hear such a prayer and grant our request? We can hope not. He says at times, "Do *not* pray for this people nor offer any plea or petition for them."[12] We need to follow *God's* directions for prayer.

We *can* still pray for people we don't know, but we should ask God to use the sickness to bring about repentance if there's sin, and a deeper walk and healing if there's no underlying sin. If we want to pray more specifically than that, we'll need to get more information, more insight, more familiarity with the situation. Quick, lazy, uninformed prayers are not meaningful to a God who's concerned about every hair on that sick person's head—and every sin in his heart.

Dealing with Those We Don't Know

What about those people whom we don't know at all but whom we merely read about or hear about?

At this level we know nothing about a situation except for a "sound bite"—a summary, a newspaper or magazine article, a spot on radio or television. We're asked to give money or pressured to pray. Best-selling books have based some of their theology and impact on these kinds of uninvestigated "stories." Here's where we should exercise great caution.

An article accuses someone of sin. Did he do it? Or is he innocent? I don't know. You don't know. The writer of the article doesn't know either. How many times have people said, "Can you *believe* the situation with that pastor?" The only appropriate answer for most of the people on this planet is, "I don't even *know* the situation. I don't think I'm called to know. Maybe we'd better leave it with God."

If it's almost impossible to discern discipline and punishment in our acquaintances, it is impossible to discern it in most (if not all) of the people we don't know. This should make us very cautious about claiming that God, for example, is punishing some politician, pastor, movie star, or person accused of a crime.

Depending on whom we listen to, we could have an accurate view of the situation, a partly-true/partly-false view of the situation, or a completely erroneous view of the situation. And we'll probably never know which.

I can know clearly in my own life what God is doing. If we're close, I can know about you. But if I don't know you, I must suspend judgment and avoid drawing conclusions. My goal should be no unsupportable ideas about God or situations. I must either settle for uncertainty about the situation, or be willing (if appropriate) to dig in and get more facts so I can "make a right judgment."

We can understand how to apply these two huge concepts of discipline and punishment in our relationships. These principles are so important that they should sober our thinking, and the details of life are so unclear that we should proceed with great caution.

If our friends are being disciplined, our path is clear. If they're being punished, our path is also clear.

It's *seeing* the difference that *makes* all the difference.

NINETEEN

*Although the Lord gives you the bread of adversity and the water
of affliction . . . your ears will hear a voice behind you, saying,
"This is the way; walk in it."*
Isaiah 30:20–21

Walking in Victory

The brightest crowns that are worn in heaven
have been tried, and smelted, and polished, and glorified
through the furnace of tribulation.

Edwin Hubbell Chapin

What on earth am I doing here?"

He looked through the lattice to the street below. People
were beginning to mill around, going into some shops, standing cautiously outside of others. He saw one boy of about
twelve quickly pocket a piece of fruit from a street vendor.

"A normal day," he thought. "For them. But not for me."

He walked around the room, which had become a beautiful prison. Sunlight poured in, causing the light colors of the
plush furniture to shine. He watched the dust particles in a
broad beam, as though he had never seen that sight before.

"That's how I feel, God" he mused. "A little piece of dust
caught, and not able to escape."

It hadn't always been so.

He thought back to when he'd first come to this exquisite
city. So scary! But what an opportunity had come to him. He
had been brought into public service and put into a three-year
leadership training program. All expenses paid, luxurious living, the best food, good friends who shared his love for God,
and days full of reading and studying. At the end of the

program, he was interviewed at the capitol and invited to be a top government advisor. He was on the fast track, and his career was in high gear.

As with most highly-visible jobs, he had been pressed to compromise his convictions. One test had come at the start of the three-year program, but he'd come through it with his integrity intact and even more respect from his superiors. Later, when the political leadership was struggling with its vision of the future and threatening a "housecleaning," he and several of his colleagues had risen to the test, asked God for guidance, and clearly laid out the possibilities for their boss. Instead of being terminated, he had been promoted to one of the top jobs in the city.

Major trials, but they had led to improvements in his career. He had come to see how God worked, rewarding perseverance. But now this! His boss, without notice, had issued a bizarre ultimatum: To continue working for him, his officials had to publicly adopt his religious views. The boss wanted "unity" with him on matters of religion and philosophy. He had refused and was now about to go to a tough exit interview with his explosive leader.

He heard a knock at the door and saw an old friend stick his head in. "Let's go, Han," his companion said somberly.

Han looked down at the street one more time and wondered what the next few hours would bring. He sighed, turned back toward the door, and walked the short distance to the capitol with his friend.

The interview went badly. The boss was even worse, even more full of rage, than Han had feared. He and his friends were ordered to "sign on" with the rest of their colleagues, but the three of them refused. Again the question "what am I doing here?" echoed through his mind. He felt numb as the boss's words rang out in fury. Han heard his own voice, sounding like a stranger, refusing one last time to compromise his convictions.

Their boss, who had treated them so well for so long, now looked at them with hatred. He ordered them to be escorted out of the room. Han felt himself being manhandled by several people who had been standing behind him.

A few minutes later, he stood before the greatest horror he had ever seen and knew he was about to go into it. He flinched but never said a word.

Bound hand and foot, Shadrach—Han to his friends—was thrust without mercy into the roaring flames.

Few of us have faced anything so fearsome as three friends faced on a long-ago day in the elegant capital city of Babylon.

After proving themselves over and over in their excellent service to their boss, King Nebuchadnezzar, it was all discounted in one act of madness by the deluded and tyrannical king. He set up a golden image ninety feet high and nine feet wide (no small goals for this man) and insisted that everyone believe the way he did, the way he said, the way he *commanded*.

A few good men refused.

They were cast into the flames and, "firmly tied, fell into the blazing furnace."[1] The fire was so hot that the men who pitched them in were themselves killed.

But the three men, facing the fiery trial to end all fiery trials, weren't even scorched. They got up and walked around in the furnace. They walked right through the fire. And they walked through it with a Friend, who didn't appear in all His glory until they had already stood their ground and been thrust into the furnace.

The fire had to be a scene out of a horror movie—but it didn't burn them at all. Nothing. Smoke in a restaurant can cling to our clothes, but these men didn't even smell like they'd been in a fire.

The only thing the fire did was to burn away the ropes that bound them.

This is the way it is with us. When we face the furnace of affliction, we can be terrorized by what we see and hear and feel. Trials can come at us from directions we never even imagined, and with greater force than we ever thought we could withstand.

But if it's the refining fire of discipline, we can be assured that we'll come through it even better, even stronger, even promoted (as Shadrach and his two friends were after their memorable experience) *if* we persevere. The fire won't destroy us, but, as with these three men, it *will* drop the fetters from our arms and legs. "He who has suffered in his body is done with sin."[2]

If instead, it's the consuming fire of punishment, we want to work humbly and closely with God to stop our offensive ways. We don't want, and don't need, to face this kind of fire.

This topic has been on my heart for a long time. *You* have been on my heart as I've written this book. I've tried to picture you, wrestling with these issues, looking for truth, hoping for help. I've tried to write this book to you, the actual person reading these words.

Seeing these principles of discipline and punishment and learning the difference between the two has revolutionized the way I look at the Scriptures, at life, at my own walk, at others, and at relationships. As you absorb God's glorious truth on these crucial areas, I'm hopeful that the same will happen for you. *You don't ever have to respond to the pain of discipline and punishment in the "old" ways again.*

God is our Father, a good and loving Abba, who longs to see you and me grow into maturity and grow out of sin. He's always working to make us better. He always makes sense, when we look at things from His perspective. And He never brings disappointment when we see His hand in it. When we understand who He is, what He's trying to do, and what His purpose for pain really is, we can—amazingly—even find ourselves being grateful for the fire.

And you *can* know these things. You *can* understand God, because He wants you to and gives you the tools to do it. You *can* see the refining fire and the consuming fire, and respond to them rightly. You don't have to be a "victim" of God's fire. You can, with His help, *use* the fire to become a praiseworthy part of a largely floundering human race. You can look up and see Him in the fire with you, walking you through the roaring flames.

When you're being disciplined, may you see it and respond well, persevering, full of joy, growing to maturity and completeness. When you're being punished, may you also see it clearly and respond well, stopping, changing course, and returning to joy. And may you always see the difference.

Grace and peace be yours in abundance.

❦

NOTES

Introduction

[1]Ps. 85:8; unless otherwise noted, all Scripture quotations are from the New International Version. [2]Prov. 3:32.

Chapter 1: The Fatherhood of God

[1]Job 5:18 [2]Lam. 3:32 [3]Ps. 23:4 [4]Phil. 3:12 [5]Ps. 103:14 [6]Josh. 3:4.

Chapter 2: Some First Principles of Suffering

[1]James Dobson, *When God Doesn't Make Sense* (Wheaton: Tyndale House Publishers, 1993), 96–97. [2]Dobson, 236–37. [3]Heb. 11:1 [4]Dobson, 8. [5]Matt. 7:7–8 [6]Jer. 29:13 [7]Dobson, 8. [8]2 Pet. 1:4; Dobson, 9. [9]Ps. 25:14; Deut. 30:11–14; Acts 17:28; 1 John 2:20 [10]Isa. 30:21 [11]Heb. 12:5 [12]Heb. 12:6.

Chapter 3: The Fire of God

[1]James 1:2, emphasis added [2]2 Tim. 2:3 [3]2 Cor. 6:10, emphasis added [4]1 Cor. 6:12 [5]Heb. 12:11, emphasis added [6]James 1:2 [7]Gal. 6:7 [8]1 Pet. 4:17 [9]Joel 2:13 [10]Lam. 3:39–40 [11]Deut. 30:11, 14 [12]Matt. 16:27 [13]Dobson, 183, 193–94 [14]Num. 14:33, emphasis added [15]1 Cor. 10:6 [16]Prov. 19:25 [17]Ezek. 18:4 [18]Ps. 36:2 [19]Prov. 10:3 [20]Heb. 2:1 [21]Eph. 5:15 [22]Ps. 119:165 [23]1 Cor. 10:12 [24]John 20:29, emphasis added [25]Prov. 29:1.

Chapter 4: Jesus and Discipline

[1]Heb. 2:14, 17, emphasis added [2]Ps. 91:14–15.

Chapter 5: God's Willingness to Discipline

[1]Isa. 48:10 [2]Luke 6:22–23 [3]John 16:33 [4]Prov. 5:21 [5]2 Pet. 2:9 [6]Ps. 34:19, emphasis added [7]2 Tim. 3:12, emphasis added [8]Prov. 16:32 [9]Heb. 11:35, emphasis added [10]2 Cor. 12:7; 11:23–29.

Chapter 6: Ten Purposes of Discipline

[1]Ps. 119:71 [2]John 15:5; 1 Cor. 10:12 [3]2 Cor. 12:7–10 [4]Heb. 2:18, emphasis added [5]Phil. 4:13, emphasis added [6]Eph. 5:15 [7]Rom. 7:21 [8]1 Pet. 4:1–2 [9]1 Pet. 4:1 [10]Mal. 3:2–4 [11]Isa. 48:10 [12]Mark 9:49, emphasis added [13]John 2:17 [14]Prov. 16:32 [15]Rom. 5:3 [16]2 Cor. 10:4 [17]2 Kings 6:16 [18]Rom. 8:17, emphasis added [19]Rev. 21:4 [20]Deut. 8:2–3 [21]Rom. 8: 32; Ps. 46:1 [22]Rom. 8:18, emphasis added [23]2 Cor. 4:17.

Chapter 7: Seven Wrong Responses to Discipline

[1]1 Cor. 10:10 [2]Prov. 19:3.

Chapter 8: Four Consequences of Responding Wrongly to Discipline

[1]Heb. 12:13 [2]Prov. 12:1 [3]Prov. 13:12, 13:4, emphasis added [4]Prov. 15:32 [5]Prov. 10:17 [6]Gal. 4:15 [7]1 Pet. 4:12 [8]John 16:33, emphasis added.

Chapter 9: The Right Response to Discipline

[1]Heb. 12:11 [2]Matt. 20:22; Luke 9:23 [3]Heb. 11:1 [4]Heb. 12:10–11, emphasis added [5]Heb. 11:6, emphasis added [6]1 Thess. 5:16–18, emphasis added [7]Job 13:15, 2:9 [8]Phil. 2:14, emphasis added [9]1 Cor. 10:10, emphasis added [10]Gal. 6:9, emphasis added [11]Heb. 12:12–13 [12]1 Cor. 9:25–27 [13]2 Tim. 2:3 [14]2 John 8 [15]1 Pet. 1:18 [16]1 Cor. 6:12 [17]Ps. 41:1 [18]Jude 22 [19]Heb. 12:13 [20]Rom. 16:20 [21]Dan B. Allender, *The Wounded Heart* (Colorado Springs: NavPress, 1990), 14, 173, 183–84.

Chapter 10: Jesus and Punishment

[1]2 Pet. 2:9 [2]2 Cor. 5:21 [3]Ezek. 18:4; Deut. 24:16.

Chapter 11: Seven Purposes of Punishment

[1]Jer. 30:11 [2]Lam. 3:47; Gen. 6:3 [3]Jer. 4:18 [4]Jer. 2:30 [5]Rom. 3:10 [6]Luke 12:47–48; 1 Tim. 1:13 [7]Ps. 19:12 [8]Gal. 6:7, emphasis added [9]2 Cor. 9:6 [10]Prov. 6:10–11; 11:25 [11]Prov. 11:31, emphasis added [12]Ps. 73:18–19; Ps. 37:10 [13]1 Pet. 4:19 [14]Mal. 3:8 [15]Isa. 26:9–10 [16]Prov. 19:25 [17]Isa. 38:15–17 [18]Prov. 12:6; 28:12; 28:15; 29:2 [19]Prov. 11:8, 10, 21; 28:10, 28 [20]Luke 17:1–2.

Chapter 12: Seven Wrong Responses to Punishment

[1]Jer. 6:14–15 [2]Heb. 12:5 [3]Gen. 31:2; 32:7, 11, 20 [4]Prov. 27:12 [5]Lev. 19:2, 1 Pet. 1:15–16, emphasis added [6]Rom. 8:4, 2 Pet. 1:3–4 [7]Luke 18:9 [8]Isa. 30:9–10, [9]Mic. 2:11 [10]Prov. 29:1 [11]Isa. 30:12–13.

Chapter 13: Ten Consequences of Responding Wrongly to Punishment

[1]Isa. 66:2 [2]Ezra 9:6 [3]2 Tim. 3:13 [4]Prov. 28:1 [5]1 John 4:18; Heb. 2:15 [6]Luke 8:17; Prov. 26:26 [7]Jer. 2:19 [8]Ps. 32:3 [9]Prov. 14:30 [10]Rom. 6:23 [11]Prov. 5:11 [12]Heb. 10:31 [13]Ps. 14:1; 10:11–13; 2:4–5; 37:13 [14]Ps. 1:1, emphasis added [15]Isa. 28:22, emphasis added [16]Prov. 23:4, [17]Ps. 90:10, emphasis added [18]Heb. 10:30; 1 Pet. 4:17; Luke 12:48 [19]Num. 14:34 [20]Ps. 90:11 [21]Rom. 9:18 [22]Ps. 76:10 [23]Rom. 2:5 [24]Heb. 12:25 [25]Isa. 26:11 [26]Exod. 24:17, [27]Deut. 4:24 [28]Deut. 28:34; 58–63 [29]Amos 3:6 [30]Zech. 3:1–2 [31]Heb. 12:28–29.

Chapter 14: The Right Response to Punishment

[1]James 1:14–15 [2]Hos. 7:14 [3]Rom. 13:7–8 [4]Col. 2:23 [5]Phil. 3:13–14 [6]Ps. 66:18 [7]2 Pet. 1:3 [8]Heb. 12:4 [9]Ps. 119:133.

Chapter 15: God's Reluctance to Punish

[1]Neh. 9:17 [2]Rom. 2:4 [3]Rom. 9:22 [4]2 Sam. 14:14 [5]1 Tim. 6:19 [6]Jon. 4:2, emphasis added [7]Ps. 103:10 [8]2 Pet. 3:9 [9]Exod. 32:12 [10]Prov. 3:32; Amos 3:7, emphasis added [11]Gen. 18:25 [12]Jer. 10:24 [13]Judg.10:16 [14]Ps. 25:7 [15]Ps. 51:5.

Chapter 16: Learning the Difference between Discipline and Punishment

[1]James 1:2–4 [2]Prov. 11:10 [3]Job 1:8 [4]Job 2:11–13, emphasis added [5]Job 42:7–8 [6]Job 5:17; 11:14; 22:23 [7]Josh. 7:6–7 [8]Josh. 7:10–12 [9]Rom. 8:7 [10]Rom. 7:17 [11]1 John 5:4 [12]2 Pet. 2:19 [13]2 Tim. 4:7–8 [14]1 Cor. 9:27 [15]Ps. 32:5 [16]Eccl. 5:18.

Chapter 17: Applying the Principles in Families

[1]This topic is discussed more fully in my book *Proactive Parenting: The Only Approach That Really Works* (Eugene: Harvest House Publishers, 1993), 51–78 [2]1 Sam. 3:13 [3]1 Kings 1:6 [4]Prov. 20:11 [5]Col. 2:23 [6]1 Sam. 23:15–18 [7]Gal. 6:2, 5 [8]Heb. 12:11 [9]Rom. 12:15 [10]Phil. 4:14; 2 Cor. 1:7 [11]James 1:5.

Chapter 18: Applying the Principles with Friends and Acquaintances

[1]2 Tim. 2:3, emphasis added [2]2 Cor. 4:16–17 [3]Heb. 10:38 [4]Prov. 17:17 [5]John 15:13 [6]Prov. 27:5–6 [7]2 Cor. 11:29 [8]Jer. 6:14; Rom. 3:4 [9]1 Tim. 4:16 [10]Luke 10:25–37 [11]Prov. 28:9; see also Isa. 1:15 [12]Jer. 7:16; 11:14, emphasis added.

Chapter 19: Walking in Victory

[1]Dan. 3:23 [2]1 Pet. 4:1.

APPENDIX
Scriptures for Further Study

Chapter 1: The Fatherhood of God

Who Is This Abba?: Isa. 64:8; Jer. 31:7–9; John 1:12–13; Rom. 8:13–17; Gal. 4:4–7; 1 John 3:1; John 2:13–17; Exod. 20:5–6; 34:6–7; Deut. 32:39; Isa. 19:22; 2 Cor. 12:9–10; Isa. 40:1–2; 2 Cor. 1:3–7; Ps. 69:26.

No Peace without Fire: Isa. 9:6; Matt. 10:34–38; Luke 12:49–53; Isa. 48:10; Zech. 13:9; Mal. 3:2–4; Matt. 3:11–12; Rev. 3:19; Deut. 4:23–24; Mal. 4:1; Heb. 12:28–29; Mark 9:49; John 14:27; 16:33.

Together in the Fire: Isa. 43:2; Dan. 3:24–27; Isa. 40:11; John 10:1–18; Rev. 7:17.

Our Firm and Loving Papa: Deut. 8:2–5; Prov. 3:11–12; Heb. 12:7–10; Isa. 49:14–16; Ezek. 18:30–32; Luke 19:41–44; 2 Pet. 3:9.

The God of Balance: Isa. 45:19; 49:14–16; Matt. 12:20; Rom. 2:4–6; 2 Pet. 3:3–12; Deut. 7:21.

Chapter 2: Some First Principles of Suffering

Let God Be True: The Word of God: Ps. 12:6; 18:25; 119:140; 2 Cor. 1:20. Faith: Isa. 7:9; Mark 9:23; 11:24; Rom. 4:18–24; 2 Cor. 5:7; Gal. 2:20; Heb. 10:35–39; 11:6; James 1:6–8.

We Can Know and Understand God: Deut. 4:29; Ps. 25:14; Prov. 3:32; Isa. 45:19; Jer. 9:23–24; Jer. 24:7; 29:13; John 17:24–26; 1 Cor. 1:18–2:16; 1 John 2:13; 5:20.

No Chance: God gives people choices: Deut. 30:11–20; Josh. 24:15; 1 Kings 18:21; 2 Chron. 15:2; Isa. 56:4–5; Hos. 8:1–3; Matt. 18:18; Acts 6:3–4; 15:22; Phil. 1:22–26. God controlling the consequences: 2 Chron. 10:1–15; 16:7–9; 32:24–26; 34:23–28; 36:11–19; Dan. 5:18–31; Rom. 1:18–32; 2 Thess. 2:9–12. See also Job 42:2; Prov. 16:4; 19:21; 21:30–31; Isa. 46:10; Dan. 4:34–35; Rom. 8:28; Eph. 1:11–12; Rev. 3:7.

Chapter 3: The Fire of God

God Is Fire: Ps. 18:8; Isa. 10:17; Ezek. 1:26–28; Dan. 7:9; 2 Thess. 1:7; Rev. 1:14–16; 4:5; Dan. 3:1–30 (example of discipline); Lev. 10:1–3 (example of punishment).

The Fire of Discipline: Job 5:7; Ps. 90:10.

Hardships Are Integral to the Christian Life: Matt. 10:17–39; John 16:33; 2 Tim. 2:1–7; 3:12; Heb. 12:2–3.

Sources of Painful Trials: Persecution: 2 Tim. 3:12. Loss: Phil. 2:25–30. Bad decisions: Prov. 11:15 (example). Facing the truth: Eccles. 1:18; 7:4. Being alive: 2 Cor. 6:10. The evil one: Job 1:6–12; 2:1–7; 1 Pet. 5:8–9; Rev. 2:10.

The Invitation of Discipline: Prov. 3:11–12; Rom. 5:3–5; Heb. 12:11; James 1:2–4.

The Fire of Punishment: Christians punished: Ps. 89:30–33; Heb. 10:26–31; 1 Pet. 4:17. Ahab and Jezebel: 1 Kings 21:17–26; 22:37–38; 2 Kings 9:30–37. Eli: 1 Sam. 2:27–33. The Jews: Acts 13:18. Canaanites: Gen. 15:16. Sin reaching its limit: 2 Chron. 36:15–16; Matt. 23:32; 1 Thess. 2:16.

Punishment Is Built into Life: The example of war: Deut. 28:45–52; Isa. 1:18–20; Dan. 5:22–31 (Babylon punished); Zeph. 2:13–15 (Assyria punished); 2 Kings 17:7–23 (Israel punished); 2 Chron. 36:15–20 (Judah punished). Innocent people suffer: Exod. 20:5–6; Num. 14:26–35. See also Ezek. 18:14–20.

Sources of Punishment: Sin: 1 Cor. 11:27–30; James 4:17. Pride: Prov. 16:18; Rev. 3:17–18. Willful ignorance: Prov. 22:3; Hos. 4:6; Folly: Prov. 19:3. Lack of faith: Mark 6:5–6; Rom. 14:23.

The Invitation of Punishment: Deut. 30:11–20; Rom. 6:1–14; Eph. 5:3–20; Titus 2:11–12.

Chapter 4: Jesus and Discipline

He Will Come: Pss. 22:5; 27:13–14; 34:17–19; Lam. 3:19–25; Heb. 10:35–39; Rev. 22:20.

Chapter 5: God's Willingness to Discipline

Forming Fire: Ps. 119:71; Rom. 5:3–5; Heb. 2:10.

Finishing Fire: Isa. 64:8; Jer. 18:1–6; James 1:2–4; 1 Pet. 1:6–7.

Pain Is an Ally: Matt. 11:28–30; Ps. 34:19; Prov. 17:3; Zech. 13:9; 1 Thess. 3:1–4; 1 Pet. 1:6–7; 4:12–13.

All of Life Is a Testing Ground: Deut. 8:1–5 (example); Heb. 11:17–19. Be ready: Mark 11:12–14 (example); 2 Tim. 4:2; Matt. 25:1–13; Mark 13:32–37.

Some Trials May Go Away; Some May Not: Deliverance: Pss. 27:1–6; 31:19–20; 32:6–7; 33:18–19; 34:1–22; 37:39–40; 72:12–14; 91:1–16; 121:1–8; Prov. 20:22; 2 Cor. 1:10–11; Phil. 1:19; 2 Tim. 4:17–18; 2 Pet. 2:9.

Discipline: God's Unchanging Plan for People: Joseph: Gen. 45:4–8; 50:15–21. Moses: Exod. 2:11–15; 10:24–29; 32:17–34. David: 1 Sam. 16:1–13; 17:28–29; 18:6–29; 19:1–12; 20:1–42; 2 Sam. 6:16–23. Paul: 2 Cor. 11:23–29; 12:7.

Chapter 6: Ten Purposes of Discipline

1. To Teach Us to Listen to God: Ps. 81:8; Isa. 55:2–3; Jer. 6:10; Mark 9:7; Heb. 3:7–8; Exod. 3:1–6.

2. To Show Us Our Frailty: Luke 12:16–20; James 4:13–16; Ps. 16:2; 103:14; Isa. 26:12; 40:6–7; Ps. 46:1; Isa. 40:28–31.

3. To Drive Out Unruliness and Bring Order into Our Lives: 1 Cor. 14:33; 40; Col. 2:5; Jer. 31:18; Ps. 119:59; Prov. 14:8; Hag. 1:5; 7; 1 Cor. 10:23.

4. To Help Us Avoid Being Condemned with the World: Rom. 7:14–8:14; 1 Cor. 11:32; 1 Pet. 4:1–2.

5. To Bring Fire into Our Hearts: Zech. 13:9; Matt. 3:11–12; Luke 12:49; Rom. 12:1; Exod. 16:4; Deut. 8:2; 26; 1 Chron. 29:17; Prov. 17:3; Matt. 5:13; Phil. 1:21; 3:7–8.

6. To Help Us Develop Perseverance and Maturity: Acts 14:22; Rom. 5:3–5; James 1:2–4.

7. So We Can Win Great Victories: Heb. 11:32–34; Isa. 26:12; James 5:17–18; 2 Kings 6:8–23; Ps. 118:15; 1 Cor. 15:57; 1 John 4:4; 5:4.

8. So We Can Enter Fully into Christ's Experience: Heb. 2:17; 1 Pet. 2:19–25; Phil. 3:10–11; Rom. 8:17.

9. So We Will Long for a Better Country: Heb. 11:9–10, 13–16, 24–26; Isa. 55:1–2; John 6:35; Phil. 3:7–8; Ps. 31:19; Prov. 11:31; Mark 10:29–30; Rom. 8:19–23.

10. To Bring Glory to God: Rom. 8:17–18; 2 Cor. 4:16–18; 1 Pet. 1:6–7.

Chapter 7: Seven Wrong Responses to Discipline

1. Ceasing to Live for God: Mark 4:16–17; Matt. 21:1–11; 26:47–56; 27:15–26; Mark 16:1; John 19:25–27; 1 Cor. 15:58; Gal. 6:9; Phil. 4:13.

2. Avoiding and Denying Pain: 1 Thess. 5:19; Isa. 30:10–11; Jer. 6:14; Exod. 32:21–24 (example); 1 Sam. 15:13–15 (example); Isa. 28:15–19; Luke 12:2; Gal. 6:7; Prov. 14:8; Ps. 139:23–24; Jon. 1:1–17; Gen. 22:1–18; Rom. 4:11–12; Heb. 11:17–19.

3. Growing Weary and Losing Heart: Isa. 49:14 (example); Gal. 6:9; Heb. 10:35–39; 12:2–3; James 1:12; Eph. 3:13; 1 Thess. 3:1–4; 1 Cor. 1:8; 2 Cor. 1:3–11; 2 Tim. 4:16–18.

4. Numbing the Pain: Jer. 46:11; Hos. 5:13; 1 Sam. 16:14–16 (example); Eccles. 2:1–11 (example); Amos 6:1–7 (example).

5. Making Excuses for God: Isa. 46:8–13; Jer. 29:11; Matt. 7:9–11.

6. Grumbling and Complaining: Num. 11:1–3 (example); 14:26–32 (example); Job 33:13–14; 35:2–3 (example); 1 Cor. 10:10.

7. Blaming God: Gen. 3:12 (example); Exod. 17:7 (example); Deut. 1:27 (example); Isa. 45:9–12; Prov. 19:3; Isa. 8:21–22; Job 38:2.

Chapter 8: Four Consequences of Responding Wrongly to Discipline

1. We Will Get Sterner Discipline: Prov. 15:10; 1 Cor. 10:12; Heb. 2:1; 2 John 8; Prov. 12:1.

2. We Will Come to Poverty and Shame: Prov. 13:4, 12, 18; 15:32.

3. We Will Lead Others Astray: Prov. 10:17; Deut. 12:31; Prov. 16:27; James 3:5–6.

4. We Will Die: Prov. 5:11–14; 21–23; 15:10; 21:16; Eph. 2:1; 1 Tim. 5:6; Rev. 3:15–16.

Chapter 9: The Right Response to Discipline

Introduction: Complaining to God: Ps. 142; Hab. 1:2–4; 1:12–2:1. Complaining about God: Num. 11:1–3; 1 Cor. 10:10; Phil. 2:14.

God's Device for Hindrance Elimination: Seeing God's hand: Ps. 73:13–17, 21–22; 119:50; Isa. 50:10; Rom. 8:38–39; 2 Cor. 5:7; Heb. 11:27.

How Long, O Lord? And How Tough? Pss. 91:10; 121:7; Prov. 12:21; Eph. 6:10–13. Crying out to God: Pss. 61:1–4; 73:25–26; 102:1–28; 130:1–8; 142:1–7; 2 Cor. 1:8–11; 2 Tim. 4:16–18; 1 Cor. 10:13.

Pain Now or Pain Later: Num. 13–14; Luke 19:41–44; Rom. 14:23.

A Condition of Deliverance: Ps. 41:1; 1 Cor. 12:26; Gal. 6:2; Heb. 3:13.

The Pain Will Be Worth It: Rom. 8:18; 2 Cor. 4:17; Acts 20:22–24; Heb. 11:13–16; 12:2–3; James 5:7–11.

Chapter 10: Jesus and Punishment

Matt. 26:47–27:56; Mark 14:43–15:41; Luke 22:47–23:49; John 18:1–19:37; Isa. 53:4–12; Rom. 2:5–11; John 3:13–18; 12:23–33; Titus 2:11–14; 1 Pet. 2:24.

Chapter 11: Seven Purposes of Punishment

Punishment Can Be an Ally—Up to a Point: Deut. 4:30; Neh. 9:26–27; Ezek. 18:30–32; Hos. 5:14–15; 1 Cor. 5:4–5; 1 Tim. 1:20.

1. To Turn Us Away from Wrong Paths: Examples of God "turning up the heat": Josh. 7:1–2; Judg. 3:7–9; 3:12–15; 2 Chron. 33:10–13; Ps. 78:32–35; 1 Cor. 5:1–5. See also Zeph. 3:7–8.

2. To Cut Out and Kill the Cancer in Our Hearts: Gen. 15:16; Matt. 23:32; 1 Thess. 2:16; Isa. 1:21–28; Dan. 4 (example).

3. To Cleanse and Purge Our Hearts: Prov. 20:30; Luke 12:47–48; Acts 3:17–20; Pss. 19:12; 139:24; 51:1–19.

4. To Teach Us the Reap/Sow Principle: Acts 8:26–40; Josh. 10:1–15; Gen. 5:24; 2 Kings 2:1–12; Gal. 6:7; 2 Cor. 9:6; Prov. 11:21; Eccles. 3:17.

5. To Let Justice Reign in the Universe: 2 Pet. 2:9; Jude 14–15; Prov. 11:31; 1 Pet. 4:19; Matt. 5:38–42; Rom. 12:19. *Lex talionis:* Exod. 21:23–25; Lev. 24:19–20; Deut. 19:21. Achan: Josh. 7. Ananias and Sapphira: Acts 5:1–11. Judas: John 12:4–6; Matt. 27:5.

6. To Teach People Righteousness: Isa. 26:9–10; Prov. 19:25. Examples: Deut. 19:16–20; Jon. 1:1–16; Acts 5:1–11; 19:13–17.

7. To Protect the Innocent: Exod. 22:22–24; Pss. 10:12–18; 18:4–24; 37:1–40; 59:1–17; 109:1–31; Prov. 22:22–23; 23:10–11; Jer. 21:12.

Chapter 12: Seven Wrong Responses to Punishment

1. Denying: Pss. 10:11–13; 14:1; 94:7–11; Jer. 2:34–35; Amos 9:10; 1 John 1:8, 10; Luke 12:16–21 (example); Jer. 23:14–22; Matt. 23:25–28.

2. Hiding: Isa. 28:15–19; 30:1–7; 31:1–3; Obad. 3–4; 2 Thess. 2:9–12; Ps. 139:7–12.

3. Losing Heart: Heb. 12:5; Deut. 28:65–67; Jon. 4:1–9 (example); Gen. 31–32 (Jacob); Joel 2:11–14.

4. Ignoring: Ps. 36:1–4; Rom. 1:18–2:5; Heb. 10:26–31; 2 Pet. 3:3–7; Prov. 1:20–33.

5. Justifying: Exod. 34:6–7; Num. 14:18; 1 Pet. 1:14–16; 1 Cor. 15:33.

6. Comparing: Luke 18:9–14 (example); 1 Cor. 11:1; 2 Cor. 10:12; Gal. 6:4.

7. Becoming Stiff-necked: Prov. 6:12–15; 29:1; Acts 7:51; Matt. 15:8–9; 1 Thess. 5:3. Pharaoh: Exod. 3:18–22; 11:1–11; 14:1–31. Belshazzar: Dan. 5:1–31. Herod: Acts 12:21–23.

Chapter 13: Ten Consequences of Responding Wrongly to Punishment

1. Direct Losses: Eccles. 2:17–26 (example); 5:10–15; Luke 16:19–31.

2. Loss of Discernment: David: 2 Sam. 11:1–27; 13:1–29. See also Matt. 6:22–23; Rom. 1:21–25; Eph. 4:17–19; 1 John 2:11.

3. Fear: Lev. 26:36–37; Deut. 28:66; Job 15:20–26; Prov. 28:1; Isa. 33:14; 1 John 4:16–18; Prov. 1:28–32; Jer. 11:11–14; Zech. 7:13.

4. Shame and Humiliation: David: 2 Sam. 16:5–14. Babel: Gen. 11:1–9. Jezebel: 1 Kings 18:4; 2 Kings 9:30–37. Nebuchadnezzar: Dan. 4:1–37. See also Prov. 6:32–35.

5. Separation and Wandering: 1 Cor. 5:1–13; Gen. 3:1–8 (example); 4:1–16 (example); Hos. 9:17; Amos 8:11–12; Eph. 2:11–12; 2 Pet. 2:15; Jude 12–13.

6. Bitterness: Job 20:12–19; Prov. 5:1–5; Eccles. 1:2 (example); Jer. 2:19; 4:1; Amos 8:10.

7. Rotting: Pss. 32:3–4; 38:1–10; Prov. 5:7–14; 14:30; Ezek. 37:11 (example); Rom. 6:23; 1 Cor. 11:27–30.

8. Judgment and Loss: Heb. 10:26–31; 1 Pet. 4:17. The Sabbath: Exod. 20:8–11; 23:12; Lev. 26:33–35; 2 Chron. 36:20–21; Jer. 29:10; Dan. 9:2; Isa. 58:13–14; Heb. 4:9–11.

9. Wrath: Ps. 2:1–6; 2:10–12; 90:11; Zeph. 3:7–8. Driven from God's presence: Gen. 3:22–24 (example); 2 Kings 17:16–23 (example). Hardening the heart: Rom. 9:18; Exod. 7:1–5 & 8:12–15 (example); Deut. 2:26–30 (example). Storing up wrath: Rom. 2:5; Hos. 13:12.

10. Consuming Fire: Deut. 4:24; Heb. 12:28–29; Isa. 5:25; 26:11. White throne: Rev. 20:11–15. Judgment of works: 1 Cor. 3:10–15.

Chapter 14: The Right Response to Punishment

Introduction: John 15:5; Rom. 6:11–14; 7:14–8:14; Gal. 5:16; Heb. 2:14–18; 4:14–16.

Wanting to Give Up Sin: James 1:13–16; Col. 3:1–6; 1 Pet. 2:11.

Living as a New Creature in Christ: Becoming a Christian: John 3:14–18. Repenting of sin: Matt. 3:1–3. Confession: Ps. 51:1–19 (example). Weeping the right way: 2 Chron. 34:14–33 (example); 2 Cor. 7:8–11. Example of restitution: Luke 19:1–10. Biblically required multiples after a theft: Lev. 6:1–5 (20%); Exod. 22:4 (times 2); Exod. 22:1 (times 4 and 5); Prov. 6:30–31 (times 7). Restitution after an injury: Exod. 21:18–19. Care of children: 1 Tim. 5:8. Relying on the Holy Spirit: Gal. 5:16. Forgetting what is behind: Phil. 3:12–14. Resisting the sinful nature; the world; and the devil: Rom. 6:11–14; 1 John 2:15–17; 1 Pet. 5:8–9.

Hope for the Person Who Truly Stops: Job 36:5–12; Ps. 32:1–5; 2 Cor. 5:14–21; Eph. 2:11–22; Col. 2:13–14; 1 John 1:9.

Taking Time: 1 Pet. 1:13–16; Heb. 12:4; James 4:1–10; 2 Pet. 1:3–4.

Chapter 15: God's Reluctance to Punish

Taking No Pleasure: Ezek. 33:10–11; Hos. 11:8–11; 2 Pet. 3:9; Luke 15:11–24; Jon. 3:1–4:11.

Better Treatment: Pss. 103:10; 130:3–4; Jer. 33:8–9; Rom. 5:6–8; 1 Tim. 1:12–17 (example).

Punishment and God's Reputation: Isa. 48:9, 11; Ps. 106:6–8; Ezek. 20:8–22; 36:16–32; Exod. 32:9–14 (example); Num. 14:10–25 (example).

Chapter 16: Learning the Difference Between Discipline and Punishment

How Will We Learn the Difference? Job: Job 1:18–22; 2:3, 10; 2:11–13. Joshua: Josh. 7:1–26. Ananias and Sapphira: Acts 5:1–11. Abigail and Nabal: 1 Sam. 25.

Self-Discipline: Rom. 6:15–23, Rom. 7:18–23, Rom 8:5–11, Gal. 5:16–21.

Self-Punishment: Ps. 130:3–4; John 8:31–36; Gal. 5:1; 1 Pet. 2:16; 1 John 1:9.

Chapter 17: Applying the Principles in Families

Applying the Principles with Children: Ps. 112: 1–2; Prov. 10:1; 11:29; 13:1; 14:26; 15:5; 17:1, 25; 19:18, 29; 20:7, 11, 30; 22:6, 15; 23:24; 29:15, 17, 19, 21; 30:17.

Applying the Principles with Spouses and Other Family Members: Encourager: Heb. 10:24–25. Helper: 2 Cor. 1:11. Fellow Sufferer: Heb. 10:32–34. Instructor: Prov. 16:21–24. Dissuader: 2 Cor. 5:20. Withdrawer: 1 Tim. 1:19–20; 2 Tim. 2:17–18; 4:9–10, 14–15.

Chapter 18: Applying the Principles with Friends and Acquaintances

Comforting the Afflicted: God able to heal: Mark 9:14–27. God willing to heal: Matt. 8:1–3; Isa. 53:4–5; Matt. 8:16–17; James 5:14–16. Abraham and Isaac: Gen. 22:1–19. See also 1 Cor. 12:26; Heb. 13:3; 1 John 3:14–18.

Afflicting the Comfortable: Luke 17:3; Gal. 6:1; 1 Thess. 5:19; Ps. 141:5; Prov. 25:12. The heart of a godly rebuke: 2 Cor. 2:1–4; 7:8–12.

Dealing with Acquaintances: Luke 10:25–37.

Dealing with Those We Don't Know: 1 Sam. 16:7.

Chapter 19: Walking in Victory

Dan. 3:1–30; Isa. 43:1–2; Ps. 66:8–12.

Mr. Lucas welcomes your comments and requests for additional information. Please contact him at:

Relationship Development Center
P. O. Box 2566
Shawnee Mission, KS 66201
913-384-7143